REVELATION: 41 QUESTIONS AND ANSWERS

REVELATION: 41 QUESTIONS AND ANSWERS

A Bible Study

Robbie Stollger

INTRODUCTION

If you have ever read through the book of Revelation, then you probably came out of it with a lot more questions than answers. You are not alone! Having studied the book a number of times personally and with different churches, I have found that the number of questions is almost endless. Between the symbolism and the Old Testament references, the book almost seems to have been written in a sort of code. In fact, that is exactly what I believe happened.

John was a prisoner of Rome on Patmos when God gave him the book of Revelation. Jesus commanded him to send the book to seven specific churches. But why would the Roman authorities allow the book off of the island, especially since it had much to say about Rome (both its present in John's day and its future)? In fact, one of the keys to the code of Revelation is a knowledge of the Old Testament, especially the books of prophecy concerned with the Kingdom. This would have been simple for the churches, which still contained plenty of Jewish believers who would recognize the symbols and references. But the Romans would likely write it off as a book of gibberish that did not really mean anything. Sadly, many professing believers today seem to share that view.

Revelation is by no means an easy book. It requires a great deal of prayer, study, and research into the Old Testament. The Bible study that you hold in your hand is the result of many years of study, and it by no means answers all of the questions that come up when reading this awesome but challenging book. Some of the questions we do address are questions that I have had myself; others have been raised by church members involved in these studies. Some of the answers may not be completely correct, but all come out of a strong desire to let the Bible explain itself. I have speculated, too, from time to time, but I always try to make it clear when I am doing so. It is not wrong to consider possible explanations, as long as we do not insist on them when the Bible does not make the answer clear.

I want to warn you before you embark on this study that it will require some hard work! The meat of this study is in the Scriptures that you will be asked to read. For many of the questions, there will be an extensive list of them. PLEASE read them carefully, prayerfully, and more than once whenever necessary. Look for common words and descriptions as you compare the Scriptures with one another. Let God's Word be your most important guide as you seek to understand the Bible's final book. And please consider my answers only after you have meditated on the Word. (And do not forget to read those listed within the answers as well!) If there seems to be any discrepancy between my answers and God's Word, then do not hesitate to believe God's Word every time! But understand that any difference between the two is not an intentional departure from Scripture on my part, but simply the mark of one who is himself still very much learning what to make of this intriguing prophecy.

It would be helpful if you would use the New American Standard Bible as you make your way through this study, as that is the version upon which I have based what I have written. If you do not have a copy of your own, you can read it online at sites such as www.crosswalk.com. There are a number of really good translations, but the NASB is one of the most literal in regard to the original languages, which is a big help when seeking to understand what God wants to communicate to us.

This Bible study is made up of 41 questions with answers, plus a handful of what I call Flashbacks. These Flashbacks will allow us to look a little more in-depth at some of the background information that should help us to understand the individual studies a little better. It covers most, but not all, of the chapters in Revelation, but it will certainly not even begin to answer all of the questions that you may have. In fact, it is likely that more questions will occur to you as you study. This is a great thing! This will give you an opportunity to use the principles for Bible study that you will practice here to explore those questions on your own.

In fact, that is the second most important reason that I wanted to share this study with you. The first is, of course, to give us all a better understanding of Revelation. But the second is also very important. If we learn to study Scripture in light of the whole Bible instead of just as isolated verses, we will come to a much more complete understanding of what God is teaching us. A clearer understanding will enable to us to obey God more faithfully and to become more like Jesus. And this is the ultimate goal of Bible study, not just head knowledge, but knowledge that transforms our minds and our hearts to make us more like our Savior (Romans 12:1-2).

I am praying for you as you launch into this study. Please take your time and let God help you to understand each section before you try to move on to the next one. If you have trouble wrapping your mind around some of the Scriptures, talk to friends who are also working through the study, or better yet form a study group to do it together. God intends for our iron to sharpen the iron of others, and vice-versa (Prov. 27:17). He has made the church into a body so that none of us will be able to do all that we need to do by ourselves (1 Cor. 12); instead, we all need to be connected to each other with Christ as our head!

As you will see, God promises special blessings to those who dare to study this book. I pray that you find all of His blessings and more as you immerse yourself in this part of God's Word!

QUESTION 1

What is the book of Revelation all about?

Read Rev. 1:1, 10-20.

John tells us in the first verse of Revelation both the contents of the book and its purpose. Its purpose, he says, is to show the church things that must take place in the future. Up to this point in time, the church knew that Jesus had promised to come back, and they had been given some information about the end times events by Jesus (Matt. 24) and Paul (1 Thess. 4:13-18; 2 Thess. 2). There were also, of course, many Old Testament prophecies to consider, especially from the book of Daniel.

But Revelation would provide the church with a more complete outline of the whole story, especially of the last seven years of the history of this age of the earth, also known as Daniel's 70th Week. (Some also refer to this period as the Tribulation, but Scripture never specifically calls it that. We will look at Daniel's 70 Weeks of Years Prophecy later in the study.) It also tells us more about some of the important people (and other beings) who will be involved in these events. Overall, the picture is quite dark. One might ask why God would want to frighten us with such terrible promises.

But if we think about what might happen if God chose not to warn us about the things to come, His purposes for doing so become even more clear. First, Satan's servants will, like their master, be quite clever and deceitful (Matt. 24:24). Jesus does not want His people to be confused about what is happening. Second, while these events will be very difficult for God's people, we must be prepared to endure them. Every loving parent will tell a child about some of the unpleasant aspects of, for example, getting shots so that he or she will not feel betrayed when they experience the pain. But that parent will also explain to the degree that the child can understand that this pain is actually for her long-term benefit.

Perhaps most importantly, God wants His people to know that, when these terrible things are happening, He has by no means abandoned them! God emphasizes again and again throughout Revelation His eternal nature and His complete power over His universe; the fact is that He was here before any of these things were created and will still be here long after these events have faded into the forgotten past. (Rev. 1:4-8 is just one of many examples of this emphasis.) God reminds His people throughout Scripture that He will never forsake us, and that He will one day bring all suffering and injustice to an end. While He allows those things to last, He is working to bring all of His plans to completion, especially the salvation of the lost (2 Peter 3:9).

The content of the book of Revelation is made clear by its first five words: **The Revelation of Jesus Christ** (Rev. 1:1 NASB). The word "revelation" means an unveiling, making something clear that may have been at least partially hidden at some point. So how is Jesus unveiled in Revelation?

Did you notice that when John first sees Jesus in vss. 12-17 that he does not seem to recognize Him? In fact, Jesus nearly scares His faithful disciple to death! We know that this is Jesus because of the details that are given about Him--the sharp two-edged sword that comes from His mouth (Rev. 1:16; 19:15); the fact that He had risen from the dead (vs. 18); and the reminder that He walks among the churches and holds its leaders in His hand. This is the same Jesus that John had known so well on earth; he had actually leaned on his chest at the last supper (John 13:23). But now, revealed in all of His glory and holiness, John seems almost not to recognize Him. In any case, He is frightened by His presence, which would never have been true when Jesus lived among and taught His disciples before His crucifixion.

This shows us that, while He was fully God as He walked in human flesh on the earth, much of His true glory and power was hidden from the eyes of human beings. Philippians 2:7 tells us that, in order to become a Man who could die for us, He had to at least temporarily lay aside some of His divine characteristics. I think Tolkien captured this in "The Lord of the Rings" when Aragorn, Gimli, and Legolas encountered the resurrected Gandalf in Fanghorn Forest, not knowing that he was alive again. He appeared as an old man dressed in a worn cloak, but when his cloak was cast aside, his true nature nearly blinded them.

In Revelation John saw Jesus for the first time in all of His glory. (He had seen a preview of this at the transfiguration, but not His full resurrected and ascended glory.) Revelation also means to show us Jesus as King of all kings and Lord of all lords. We will all, no doubt, be in awe as John was when we get our first sight of the fully glorified Lord Jesus Christ. But just as He did with John, He will reassure us that, because our faith is in Him, we have absolutely nothing to fear.

QUESTION 2

What is the blessing that Revelation promises to those who study it?

Read Rev.1:3; 22:7

As believers committed to the Bible as our sole source of true authority, we expect to be blessed any time that we read God's Word. But Revelation offers a special blessing to those who **read**, **hear**, and **heed** its words. Does studying Revelation give us a different kind of blessing from our studies of other Scriptures?

I think the answer to this question is both "yes" and "no." Since it is part of God's revealed Word to His people, we can expect to get all of the same blessings from studying Revelation that we do from other Scriptures. What are those blessings? They certainly include truth (which provides both knowledge and wisdom), conviction when something in our lives is not right, encouragement that God loves us and is always with us, and direction for our daily lives.

But Revelation may also offer some blessings that are not always found in other Scriptural studies, at least not to the same degree. First, Revelation gives us the clearest picture in Scripture of what will happen as the time for Christ's return draws close. As we discussed earlier, this information is crucial for the church as it prepares for the difficult times that will accompany Satan's last gasp for power. While we get some of this information from other passages, Revelation puts it together in a unique and more complete way. This seems to be the particular blessing that God has in mind, since in both passages the blessing is coupled with the reminder that these events will soon happen.

In my own personal experience, I have also received some other blessings that I think are at least somewhat unique to a study of Revelation. While I cannot say I truly enjoy reading the book because its tone is so dark and its warnings are so heavy, I do always come out of a personal or corporate study of Revelation with stronger faith, knowing that God will always be present no matter how rough the fight here on planet Earth becomes. I am reminded that He is far more powerful than any evil force in the universe, and that while He does not always step in immediately on behalf of His children, He does always arrive at exactly the right time. And I am reminded that even the worst things that we will face here on earth pale in comparison to the good things that He has in store for us in eternity (Rom. 8:18).

Finally, Revelation does something for my spiritual maturity that is difficult to find in most other studies. For lack of a better way to express it, it stretches me. I love reading the familiar passages that declare the good news of the Gospel or that encourage me about God's mercy and sustaining love for me despite my sins. I am inspired by the stories of old as I see God come through for His people to bring them victory. But Revelation is not always so encouraging and uplifting, and when we add in the fact that it can be so challenging to understand, I can see why many people would rather just ignore it altogether. I have experienced this often as a pastor. Any time I feel led to begin an end-times study, there are always at least a few people who would rather focus on something else.

The tough and dark subject matter can be a discouraging combination. We experience some of the same discouragement with physical exercise, where we often stop when we start feeling muscle pain or shortness of breath. But those things are actually evidence of how much we need to be challenging ourselves with physical activity, and when we push through and refuse to give up, then we find ourselves breathing better and hurting less in a short period of time. Studying Revelation is that same sort of exercise for our minds and our spirits. If we persevere through prayer and diligent meditation on the relevant Scriptures, we will slowly begin to see things more clearly. And, while some of the events that are prophesied will remain dark and heavy, we will also be encouraged as we see more of the light that will one day utterly overcome them (John 1:5).

Second only to a deeper understanding of this part of God's Word, my fondest wish for anyone embarking on this study is that you will become accustomed to having God stretch you through a more thorough study of His Word. Like physical exercise, it will not always seem fun, but the rewards as you gain spiritual strength and vitality will make it well worth the temporary discomfort. And I believe with my whole heart that one of the things needed most in today's church is a willingness to challenge ourselves to a deeper understanding of God and His will for us through His Word.

There is one other thing that is very important for us to see here. Rev. 1:3 offers the blessing to those who read, hear, and heed **the words of this prophecy** (NASB). Rev. 22:7 puts the emphasis squarely on the heeding. In the First Century, the scroll containing the contents of Revelation would have been shared in the churches by being read aloud to the congregation. There were no copies of Scripture to take home and study in private. The readers (likely the pastors) and the hearers (the church members) were offered this blessing, but ultimately only if they then followed through and obeyed its commands. This was the whole point of the reading and of the hearing. As James tells us, true faith *will* result in obedience to God's Word (James 1:21-25); this obedience is the only path to blessing.

QUESTION 3

What does John mean when he talks
about being "in the Spirit?"

Read Rev. 4:1-2; 2 Cor. 12:1-4

We have two options to consider in answering this question. If the Spirit here means the Holy Spirit, then John is describing a state where the Holy Spirit is literally taking his body through a door into Heaven. If spirit here means John's spirit, then he is describing his spirit and soul temporarily leaving his body and making the trip without it. When Paul was taken to visit Heaven, he did not know whether he went there physically or whether his soul/spirit visited without his body (2 Cor. 12). Apparently what he saw there was so awesome that an awareness of his physical state did not seem important!

The text of Revelation itself does not give us a clear answer, as capital letters were not used in the original Greek documents. (Modern translators often capitalize the word "spirit" when it refers to the Holy Spirit.) The word is the same, and so we have to look to the context for clues. The translators of the New American Standard leave no doubt for us that their interpretation is that the Holy Spirit took John to Heaven in his earthly body. I believe they are right based on some other passages in Revelation itself.

For example, in Revelation 5:4, John describes himself as **weeping greatly** (NASB). This would seem to indicate that he was

14

in his body. Also, in Rev. 10:4 John is taking notes, which would indicate that he was physically present. Later in that same chapter, the angel commands him to eat a small book and he obeys. In Chapter 11, he is handed a measuring rod and commanded to measure the end-times temple. All of these clues add up to John being there physically, which would mean that here that the word Spirit refers to the Holy Spirit who carries him where he needs to go.

FLASHBACK 1

Body, Soul, and Spirit

Read Gen. 2:7; 1 Thess. 5:23; 2 Cor. 5:1-9

Although this passage was almost certainly describing God's Holy Spirit, it is good for us to look for a moment at our makeup as human beings. The Bible tells us that we are made up of body, soul, and spirit (1 Thess. 5:23). This is no doubt a part of being made in the image of God, who also exists as Three in One. Gen. 2:7 tells us that after God created Adam's body, He breathed the breath of life into him. The Hebrew word for breath is also the word for spirit.

It is through our spirits that we connect with God, which means that our connection with Him is deeper than a mere physical or even mental/emotional connection. I had a friend who was hit by a car while riding his bicycle while we were both in seminary. By God's grace he was taken to the emergency room where his wife worked as a nurse, but he had no idea who she was or who he was. He had no memory of anything that had happened in his past, but he could still speak Spanish (which he had studied in preparation for mission work) and he still knew that He believed in Jesus! The Holy Spirit's conviction works at the deepest possible level in our lives and forms a bond between God and believers that can never be broken by any power of the enemy!

This three-part makeup is also important when we think about death. Some believe that death is an end, a time when we cease to exist. But the Bible never describes death in that way. In fact, the Bible says two things that might seem contradictory at first. It says that in death our bodies sleep (1 Thess. 4:13), but at the same time that we are in the conscious presence of the Lord the moment we die (Phil. 1:21-23). This would not be possible if our bodies were our entire beings as so many would have us to believe.

But because the Bible tells us that there is more than one part to who we are, we discover that while our bodies may sleep (and even decay) in death, our souls and spirits do neither! 2 Cor. 5 tells us that when we are alive, our souls and spirits are at home in our bodies. When this is true, we cannot be in the Lord's presence, since He is in Heaven. But when we die, we do not cease to exist. Instead, our souls and spirits leave our bodies and go to be with Jesus. The conscious part of who we are lives with Him in Heaven until He returns to resurrect and perfect our bodies to never die again (1 Thess. 4:13-18)! So death is not an end. It is actually a separation from our earthly lives to a Heavenly one. The souls under the altar in Heaven in Rev. 6:9 testify to this reality.

It would have been possible for Paul or John to have their souls/spirits leave their bodies and travel to Heaven, which would have been a kind of temporary death. But their bodies would have come to life again once their spirits/souls had returned. When Jesus raised Lazarus (along with several others) during His earthly ministry, this is what happened. While I do not believe that John did leave his body for the reasons described above, it is good for us to understand that these parts of who we are can be separated, at least for a time, and will be at death unless Christ returns while we are still at home here in our earthly tents.

QUESTION 4

What do you make of the description
that John gives of God the Father?

Read Rev. 4:2-3; 1 Tim. 6:13-16; 1 John 4:12;
Ex. 33:18-23

It is no surprise that as John enters Heaven's throne room his attention is immediately drawn to the central figure there-- One who sits enthroned and to whom everyone else in Heaven is completely attentive. He clearly describes a Person (using the pronoun "He" and later in Chapter 5 describing Jesus as taking something from His hand). Yet he makes no attempt to describe any form other than to say that His glory shone like the most beautiful, reflective jewels on earth. All that he puts into words are visions of beautiful colors of light.

This is, in fact, consistent with other descriptions of en- counters with God in Scripture. Both Isaiah (Isaiah 6) and Eze- kiel (Ezekiel 1) saw Him, but His face was shielded by angels and smoke or fiery clouds. Moses, who talked with Him on at least two different mountains through a burning bush and a thick cloud, begged to see God's face, but God told him that he could not survive such an encounter. When the high priest entered the holiest place on the Day of Atonement, he first burned great clouds of incense on the altar in the holy place so that he would not see God's face as he met with Him at the mercy seat atop the ark of the covenant (Lev. 16:12-13).

In the New Testament the two men who visited Heaven,

Paul and John, both testified to the fact that no living person has ever seen God's face. Paul also added, right in line with John's description here, that God **dwells in unapproachable light** (1 Tim. 6:16 NASB). It seems likely that God was hidden behind the light of His Shekinah glory so that neither man would die at that point in time, since He still had plans for them on earth.

God's children have always longed to see Him, but have never been able to do so because sinful man cannot survive a direct encounter with a holy God. But the tearing of the temple veil reminds us that this will not always be the case. And it is no accident that this happened the moment that Jesus died, making full and final atonement for our sins (Matt. 27:50-51). Now we can see God and even live with Him in Heaven when our souls and spirits leave our bodies here on earth. And after the resurrection, we will be able to be with Him in physical bodies that will never again be subject to sin or sorrow, pain or death. We truly have only just begun to taste what a relationship with God will be like for eternity (Rom. 8:18-23; 2 Cor. 5:5)!

QUESTION 5

Who are the elders enthroned
around God the Father?

Read Rev. 4:4; Rev. 3:4-5; Rev. 7:9; 2 Tim. 2:12; Rev. 5:9-10; Rev.
21:10-14

There has been much debate as to the identity of the 24
elders introduced to us in Rev. 4:4. Some have seen them as men
and others as angelic beings. And while Revelation does not give
us this answer directly, I believe that the clues that we find in vs.
4, when cross-referenced with other Scriptures, make it pretty
clear.

Notice the details given about the beings in this short
verse. They sit on thrones, indicating a certain amount of authority under God's ultimate authority. They also wear crowns which
could refer either to royal crowns, again indicating authority, or
more likely to the crown of life described in James 1:12 which
God has prepared for believers. They wear white clothing and are,
of course, called elders.

All of these indicate that these are saved human beings.
God promises believers that they will one day reign with Him
(2 Tim. 2:12). Redeemed human beings are seen repeatedly
throughout Revelation dressed in white robes. (Angels are sometimes seen wearing white as well, but for human beings the white
speaks of redemption and good deeds that accompany salvation
by God's grace through faith--Eph. 2:8-10.) Angels are not depicted wearing crowns or sitting on thrones. If the crowns are the

crown of life, then believers are definitely in view. And, finally, the word "elders" is used in Scripture to describe human beings who are entrusted with some sort of leadership authority. All of these things taken together argue strongly that these 24 elders are human beings.

If that is the case, then the next logical question is: which 24 people are they? Some have argued that they only represent saved humanity and are not historical figures at all. But I believe that Revelation itself, once again, gives us our best clue as to who these 24 men are. Describing the New Jerusalem in Revelation 21, the names of the 12 sons of Israel (namesakes of the 12 tribes) are said to be written on the 12 gates to the city, and the names of the 12 apostles are written on the 12 foundation stones. These 2 groups of 12 men are the ultimate elders of Scripture--the original elders of Israel and of the church. This may be why it was essential that Judas be replaced after his suicide (Acts 1).

Of course, if this is true, then there is one great irony to enjoy. John, who was seeing future events in Heaven, would have seen his resurrected and glorified self among them! (Some might argue against this since he did not seem to recognize himself, but remember that he also apparently did not recognize the glorified Lord Jesus Christ either.) Wouldn't it be even more ironic if the elder who speaks to him in Rev. 5:5 was his own future self?!

While we cannot be dogmatic about the identity of these elders, the evidence seems to overwhelmingly support the fact that they were human men. And if they were redeemed people and were not the 12 patriarchs and 12 apostles, it seems impossible to guess who else they might have been.

QUESTION 6

Who are the seven Spirits of God?

Read Rev. 4:5; 5:6; Rev. 1:4-5; Zechariah 3:8-10; Zech. 4:6-10; John 15:26-27; John 16:7

Probably the biggest question that I had when first beginning to study Revelation was this one: What on earth is meant by **the seven Spirits of God** (NASB)? Once again, the translators of the New American Standard Bible have tipped their hands here, capitalizing the word **Spirits**. But if this is true, why is He depicted as a group of seven Spirits rather than as just the one Holy Spirit, third Person of the Trinity? This did not seem like a small matter to me, and still does not to this day. Are we being told that the Holy Spirit is made up of seven different spirits, or is that instead an image meant to convey some truth about Him?

My first source of comfort came when I discovered that this imagery for the Holy Spirit has its roots in the Old Testament. Zechariah 3 promises the coming of the Branch, a common Old Testament description of Jesus (Isaiah 11:1; Jeremiah 23:5). The idea is that He is a branch growing out of the root of David and Jesse (David's father). The Messiah Jesus came, both through his biological mother and legal father/step-father Joseph, from David's royal line, as the genealogies in Matthew and Luke tell us.

Vines and trees were essential to life in Israel, as many of their most precious crops grew on them. The olive tree, in particular, was vitally important both as a food source and as a source of oil for cooking and fuel for lighting the home. The importance of olive oil to their lives may be the reason that

God chose to pour that oil over the heads of kings, priests, and prophets to mark them as set aside for office. This oil also served as a symbol of the Holy Spirit who would be needed to empower them for their life of service. The same imagery is used in the New Testament when people are anointed with olive oil for healing (James 5:14; Mark 6:13). The pouring out of the oil is a prayer for the Holy Spirit to fill and empower the person who is to serve or to heal one in need of healing.

As Zechariah prophesied the coming of the Branch, he also used the image of Christ as a rock with seven eyes. (Christ is referred to as a rock or stone in the New Testament also--1 Peter 2:4, 7; 1 Cor. 10:4.) Zechariah promises that on the day that God inscribes that rock--a description of the piercing of His body by nails and
spear?--He will take away all of Israel's sin. So the rock with seven eyes is Jesus. Hold that thought for just a moment.

In Zechariah 4, God is showing Zechariah that He intends to rebuild the temple through Zerubbabel, the descendant of David who led Israel at the time, although not officially as king. He would also use Joshua, who was high priest. (Zechariah prophesied after the return from captivity in Babylon when the people came home to find Jerusalem and Solomon's temple in ruins.) And He promised that two olive trees would give the temple's seven-branched menorah a continuous supply of oil. Normally, the priests had to fill it twice a day to keep it burning at all times. But God promised a future when the supply of spiritual light and power would flow continuously.

Then God tells Zechariah outright that these things would happen not by human power but by the power of His Spirit. He also identified the Holy Spirit with the seven branches of the menorah, which He again called His seven eyes.

All of this may seem confusing, but the important point for our study is this: there is a precedent in the Old Testament for the Holy Spirit to be described as a group of seven eyes or spirits. And the seven eyes are tied to Christ as the stone in Zechariah and as the Lamb in Revelation 5. But it is Revelation 1:4-5 that fully confirms that the seven Spirits here refer to the one Holy Spirit, as there the Father, Son, and seven Spirits are presented as the holy Trinity.

So if we are certain that the seven Spirits really refer to the one Holy Spirit, then why is He described as seven rather than one? I do not believe that we are being told that He is really made up of seven individual spirits. I am convinced that this is a symbol which tells us something important about His function in the world. But what is it?

We know that seven is the number of completion or perfection, since God completed His perfect world in seven days (including His day of rest). This is likely the reason that this particular number is used. But I believe that the essential clue as to why He is presented in the plural has to do with what Jesus told His disciples in John 16:7. He made an astounding statement, telling them that it was actually to their benefit that He go back to Heaven! None of them could have imagined how that might be true, but we know on this side of the cross and resurrection just what He meant. When Jesus was on earth in an earthly body, He was limited in space and time. He could only be in one place at a time physically. But the Holy Spirit, whom He said would come if He went away, is not limited. He is the eyes of the Lord moving all over the earth all at once. He can be in every believer on earth simultaneously. He has no physical limits, and so can empower every member of His church at the same time for the work that Christ left for us to do!

So picturing the Holy Spirit as seven eyes or Spirits actually demonstrates not that there are more than one of Him, but that He can be many different places at once. He is omnipresent. And picturing the seven eyes or Spirits as being connected to Jesus (as both the rock and the Lamb), reminds us that it was Jesus who sent the Holy Spirit upon His return to Heaven (John 15:26-27). I am so thankful that both the Old and New Testaments enlighten us as to why God revealed this to us in this way! And I am thankful that we have the permanent, indwelling presence of the Holy Spirit to forever be our wisdom and our

7 completion of perfection

7 branches of the Menorah

7 days in a week

7 completion of perfection

7 branches of the Menorah

7 days in a week

Revelation: 41 Questions and Answers

QUESTION 7

Who are the four living creatures?

Read Rev. 4:6-8; Isaiah 6:1-3; Ezekiel 1:4-11

As with the seven eyes/Spirits of our last study, the Old Testament also provides us with background that helps us to identify the four living creatures around the throne. While they are not exactly like either the seraphs of Isaiah 6 or the cherubs of Ezekiel 1, there are enough similarities, I believe, to firmly state that these are an order of angelic beings.

There are four of the living creatures around God's throne; four also accompany God in Ezekiel 1. Isaiah 6 does not tell us how many seraphim were present, only that there were more than one. But similar angels seem to be among God's constant attendants.

The angels in Isaiah 6 and Rev. 4 have six wings each. The angels in Ezekiel 1 have four. The angels in Isaiah and Rev. both repeatedly declare God's holiness. Ezekiel does not record any of their words. In Revelation, John sees the four angels as four different creatures resembling a man, an ox, an eagle, and a lion. Each of Ezekiel's angels has all four of those faces. The angels that Isaiah saw had their faces covered with their wings. While it does not seem that John saw exactly the same angelic beings that Ezekiel or Isaiah saw, it does seem clear that they are all some type of angel. I suppose it could be that these very special angels who attend to God change in form and appearance from time to time. But their job is one of the most awesome ones in all the universe-- to continuously praise God for who He is and for what He has done! Some of us might think that we would get bored doing that one thing all the time, but we have never seen God! When we do, we may even be almost jealous of these angelic beings who have the privilege of never leaving His presence and of singing praises to Him that will never end! *probably angels*

man

ox,

eagle

lion

*We owe God - glory, honor +
power*

QUESTION 8

*On what basis do the elders de-
clare God to be worthy?*

Read Rev. 4:9-11

**"Worthy are You, our Lord and our God, to receive glory and
honor and power; for You created all things, and because of Your
will they existed, and were created."** Rev. 4:11 (NASB)

In response to the praises of the angels, the 24 elders assume a posture of complete submission before God, falling on
their faces and throwing their crowns at His feet. In so doing,
they are acknowledging something that many people have sadly
forgotten: God is God, and we are not.

Their words of praise may seem self-evident, but they are
some of the most important words of truth that human beings
can ever utter. First, they declare God worthy. He is deserving.
We owe Him something. What do we owe Him? We owe Him
glory and honor and power (NASB). It is our duty to acknowledge
that He is God and that He is Lord--the One who has the right to
tell us what to do with our lives.

On what basis is He declared worthy? Because everything
else that exists, including us, only exists because He chose to create us. From nothing (Heb. 11:3). Nothing existed until He de-
cided to make something. And why is that important?

It is generally accepted among human beings that when
someone creates something, he or she has the right to determine
how that creation is used. We grant patents and copyrights, de-

pending on what kind of creation it is, and no one else is allowed to use this invention or song without its creator's permission. And this is true even though we are at best sub-creators. We make new things out of old things, out of things that already exist. We use things that someone else created and put them together in a new way. We arrange established words into a song or poem. We invent something using materials--metals, computer components, etc.--that others developed before us.

If human beings acknowledge that a creator is worthy of control over his or her creation, why do so many of us struggle to give God control of our lives? Why do we rebel against His lordship, seemingly on a daily basis? In fact, I believe that this is the real reason for the surge in professed atheists in our world today. Science has not even come close to disproving God's existence. The more we learn about the wonders of the universe, the clearer it becomes that it had to be designed. But if you do not want to live your life by God's plan as revealed in Scripture, the most effective way to deal with the guilt that inevitably comes is to convince yourself that He does not exist.

But He does exist. And He did create everything, including us. And so, as the elders declare, He is worthy of our worship and of our complete obedience.

Of course, we know the rest of the story. Mankind, following Satan's example, has universally rebelled against God's rightful Lordship over our lives. It began with Adam and Eve (Gen. 3), and each of us has followed in their footsteps (Rom. 3:23), trying to form our own little kingdoms where we are in charge of our own lives. We have rejected God's rightful claim to kingship over us. And we have been condemned as traitors and sentenced to death (Rom. 6:23).

But God did not leave us there. He sent His only begotten Son to take our death sentence upon Himself so that we would have the opportunity to become citizens of His Kingdom once again (John 3:16). In order to come back home where we belong, we must repent of our sin and rebellion and believe in Jesus and what He did for us on the cross (Eph. 2:8-9). In doing so, we also acknowledge once again His rightful Lordship over our lives and commit to living in obedience to Him forever. We still fail in that commitment at times, but He is faithful to forgive us and give us an endless supply of fresh starts (1 John 1:9).

But regardless of how we respond, the truth of the elders' declaration remains. He is worthy. He is the one and only rightful King.

QUESTION 9

What is the big deal about this
sealed book or scroll?

Read Rev. 5; 1 Tim. 2:5; Matt. 28:18

John is next shown a scroll in the hand of God the Father. It is sealed with seven seals. The seals serve to hold the pages closed, as well as to declare the authority of the one who sealed them. The pages of a sealed document could not be legally opened, and its directives enacted, until the one with authority declared it to be the proper time.

When Jesus talked to His disciples about His return, their most common question was, "When?" (Matt. 24:3; Acts 1:6). Jesus informed them that even He did not know the answer to that question; only the Father knew the day and the time (Matt. 24:36). This means that it is the Father's authority that has sealed these documents and that only by His authority can its contents become reality.

One of the leading angels calls out, asking who is worthy--who has the legal right--to break the seals and to open the scroll. When it appears that no one worthy is to be found, John is distraught. Why?

John and his fellow believers were enduring a time of intense persecution at the end of the 1st Century under the Roman Emperor Domitian. The other eleven apostles had all been murdered for their faith, and John (after a failed attempt on his life by the authorities) was now in prison on Patmos. John knew that all across the Roman world believers were suffering and dying for their faith. The only sure way for persecution and the other evils of the world to be stopped was for Jesus to come back. And John knew that, if this scroll could not be opened, then that could not occur.

This leads us to the contents of the scroll. What exactly is written on the front and the back of this sealed document? Many theories have been offered, ranging from a title deed to the earth to some sort of will. But I believe that the answer is much simpler than that. I believe that the scroll contains the events described in the rest of the Book of Revelation! As each seal is broken, an event (or series of events) occurs. As the seventh seal is broken, the seven trumpet judgments begin. When the seventh trumpet is blown, the seven bowl judgments are poured out. But until the first seal is broken, none of these events surrounding the return of Christ can occur. According to Old Testament prophecy, these events will occur during the last seven years of this age of earth's history, also called Daniel's 70th Week (Dan. 9:27).

If the events surrounding Jesus' return cannot take place until the seals are broken, then it is no wonder that John and the persecuted church would be moved to weep when no one worthy to do so could be found. But an elder—perhaps a glorified John himself?--steps in and tells John that there is no reason to weep. Because, even though no one was found on earth who could open the seals, God had provided His own worthy One, His only begotten Son!

Two more prophetic descriptions of Jesus are used here to show us that He is indeed the Lamb that John sees (John 1:29). The elder calls Him **the Lion from the tribe of Judah**. In Gen. 49:9-10, Judah (described as a lion) is promised that the scepter will remain in the hands of one of his descendants until **Shiloh** comes. **Shiloh** means "the One to whom it belongs." This can only describe the Lord Jesus.

He also calls the Lamb **the root of David**. Revelation refers to Jesus both as a branch growing out of the root of David and also as the root from which David had come (Rev. 22:16). This is reminiscent of Jesus' unanswered challenge to His critics, asking them how the Messiah could be both David's Lord and His descendant (Matt. 22:41-46). The only answer, of course, was for the Son of God (the root or Creator) to become man (the descendant). This had happened in the incarnation of Jesus Christ, the second Person of the holy Trinity.

The search for one who is worthy to open the scroll underlines the New Testament teaching that salvation can be found in no one other than in God's Son Jesus Christ (John 14:6). Even the location of the Lamb when John first sees Him--between the throne and the redeemed human elders--reminds us that He is the only **mediator...between God and men** (1 Tim. 2:5 NASB).

The Lamb is further seen as having seven horns, seven eyes, and a wound that indicates that He had at some point been slain. Since He appears as a Lamb, the wound may well have been a cut across his throat, as this was how lambs were slaughtered for sacrifice. The seven eyes, as we have already seen, represent the Holy Spirit, sent out by Jesus after His return to Heaven. And the seven horns echo Matt. 28:18, where Jesus declared that all heavenly and earthly authority had been entrusted to Him. Horns, used by animals for self-defense, were considered symbols of power (as we will see with the dragon and sea-beast). The fact that He wore seven, a number that speaks of perfection, indicates that He has complete power and authority--King of kings and Lord of lords!

FLASHBACK 2

"How long?"

Read 2 Chronicles 13:11; Ps. 6:3-4; 94:3; Rev. 6:9

As Jesus steps forward and takes the book, preparing to open it, Heaven breaks forth in praise. That praise contains one very important element--bowls of incense which represent the prayers of believers. Why is incense used to represent prayers? And what types of prayers might be in view here?

The altar of incense was set in the holy place in the tabernacle and temple, just outside the veil that separated it from the holy of holies where the ark of the covenant was kept. A special blend of incense was created to burn on that altar (Ex. 30:34-38), and it was not allowed to be used by anyone else. The incense was lit using coals from the altar where sacrifices were offered. The incense represented the prayers of God's people, and was burned at the two times per day set aside for prayer--evening and morning. Lighting it with coals from the altar meant that it was God's redeemed people, covered by the blood, who were praying to Him. No one could pass through the veil into the holy of holies except for the high priest, and then only once per year on the Day of Atonement. But the smoke from the incense could, meaning that God heard the prayers of His people even though they could not approach Him personally before Jesus died on the cross.

The people of Israel no doubt prayed many of the same kinds of prayers that we do today--prayers for blessing and healing and help. Prayers of praise and thanks. Prayers for loved ones and friends. But there was one particular prayer that faithful Israelites prayed often, a prayer for God to bring the Kingdom that He had promised to Israel, the Millennial Kingdom, where Israel would be the preeminent nation on earth. It was a prayer for God to put an end to sin and take up His righteous reign in Jerusalem. And prophets, priests, and kings (along with the early apostles) often prayed asking God, "How long?"

They wanted to know how long it would be before God brought His Kingdom to earth. They wanted to know how long He would continue to allow the wicked to prosper or the righteous to suffer. They wanted to know when God would put an end to repression and abuse and injustice. God did not reprimand them for asking, "How long?" But He did not give them a definitive answer, either. Instead, He insisted that they trust Him to know when the time is just right.

I believe that it is especially these "How long?" prayers that are pictured in Rev. 5:8. God has not failed to answer this very important prayer. Instead, He has stored up these prayers of faithful believers in Heaven (along with their tears in His bottle and their names in His book--Ps. 56:8), and will answer them all in one mighty moment as His judgments against Satan's kingdom begin (Rev. 8:1-6)! This underscores the clear teaching of Scripture that the prayers of God's people play an important and powerful role in His work here on earth (James 5:16).

All of us as believers sometimes ask God "how long" He will allow evil to continue and harm to come to His people and to the innocent. We should keep asking--because one day He will clearly answer, and our prayers will play a part!

QUESTION 10

What happens when the first
4 seals are broken?

Read Rev. 6:1-8; Matt. 24:1-14; Zechariah 1:7-10

The last seven years of this age of earth's history begin with the breaking of the first of the seven seals holding the end-times scroll closed. Each of the first four seals unleashes a horseman who sets some very devastating events into motion.

Some would question whether or not these are literal figures or simply symbols of war, death, etc. God showed Zechariah a group of horsemen, almost certainly angelic beings, whom He had assigned to **patrol the earth** (NASB), especially on behalf of His people Israel. While I do not believe that they correspond exactly to these four horsemen, I do think that they show us that such beings are working in the world on behalf of God and likely on behalf of the enemy as well.

Many Bible students believe that the first horseman is in fact a very specific person known throughout Scripture as anti-Christ (1 John 2:18; 2 John 1:7), the man of sin (2 Thess. 2:3-12); and the beast (Rev. 13:1-8). Jesus warned His disciples that people would come pretending to be Him in order to deceive all who would listen (Matt. 24:4-5). This first horseman rides a white horse, meaning that he has already conquered a great deal of territory (as white horses were ridden in victory parades). He wears a crown, signifying that he is a ruler and has a great deal of authority. He also carries a bow, which likely means that he leads his armies from behind the lines, as the bow was a weapon of distance and not one for hand-to-hand combat. He is in the conquering business, and this is certainly what anti-Christ will be about when he comes (Daniel 7:7-8, 19-28; Rev. 17:12-18). But he will make a peace treaty with Israel (Dan. 9:27), and this will officially mark the beginning of the end.

The next two horsemen bring war and famine to the earth, two things which often go together. (Crops and stores of food are often destroyed or stolen by invading armies during wartime.) Vs. 6 tells us that basics like wheat and barley, needed for flour to make bread, will sell for exorbitant prices. A denarius was an entire day's wage. This would be equivalent to us paying well over $100 for a jar of unground wheat containing less than the five pound bags we currently find at the grocery store! When anything is scarce, it becomes expensive, and this will certainly be the case when this horseman rides.

Are these horsemen angelic beings? Are they perhaps demons? The text does not tell us, but it does make clear that they are released to do their damage only when Jesus permits it by breaking a seal. In Rev. 9 we find demonic beings being released to wreak havoc on earth. This could be true of these horsemen as well. Jesus also mentions war and famine (along with earthquakes) as some of the early signs of the end in Matt. 24:6-8.

The final horseman is death, followed by the grave. He reaps the harvest of the previous horsemen, wiping out 1/4 of the world's population through warfare, famine, disease, and attacks by wild beasts. These plagues on mankind often work together, but never has such a large percentage of the world's population died in such a short period of time. Imagine if one out of every four people you know suddenly died! Jesus says that these are just the early labor pains. What comes after must be Hell on earth indeed!

QUESTION 11

Who are these souls and why
are they under the altar?

Read Rev. 6:9-11; Matt. 24:15-22

As the fifth seal is broken, John is shown a group of souls--people who have died and not yet received their resurrected bodies--beneath the altar. (This is likely the altar of incense in Heaven; the earthly tabernacle was built as a replica of the tabernacle that is in Heaven--Heb. 8:3-5; Heb. 9:11-12.) The text tells us that they are martyrs, killed specifically because they are believers in Christ. The first question is this: does this group include all martyrs from history, or is it only the martyrs who will be killed during the Great Tribulation? That is actually a question that we cannot answer with certainty. I assume that because it says **the souls of those who had been slain because of the word of God** (NASB) without any qualifiers that it must mean all martyrs from Abel to the Great Tribulation, but it could very well be focused only on those last days believers who will be killed at the behest of anti-Christ.

It is also not completely clear why they are under the altar. If this is the altar of incense, then it would intensify the emphasis on the incense being burned there representing the prayers of believers. They would actually be under the altar praying "live and in person." (And they *are* alive, even though not currently in physical bodies.) I believe that this is further confirmed by the fact that they are joining the chorus of believers through the ages asking the "How long?" question, specifically asking how long God will allow the persecution of the Great Tribulation to continue. His answer is quite honest and perhaps not entirely comforting-- until all of those who will give their lives for their faith have done so.

This reminds us, as should most of this Revelation study, that God does not promise us easy, comfortable lives here on earth. In fact, He promises just the opposite (John 16:33; 2 Tim. 3:12). But the comfort in Revelation is a scene like this, which promises us that our reward--being close to God Himself in eternity and honored by Him--will more than make up for any suffering, no matter how intense, that we face here on earth (Rom. 8:18).

Regardless of whether these souls include all of history's martyrs or only those from the Great Tribulation, the timing of the opening of this seal, following the progression described by Jesus in Matt. 24, does place this future event during that horrible period of history. As we will see in the next study, the events of the next seal follow directly on the heels of the Great Tribulation. So we know that, even as the martyrs ask this question, the very time that they are praying for is near.

One other insight we can gain from this passage is that what we often call Heaven is actually a work in progress. Please do not misunderstand. Heaven is a perfect place because God is there. No harm will ever again come to those who dwell there under His protection. And, because they are in His presence in a way that we can never be while on earth in our mortal bodies, they are in a place of joy that is full to overflowing (Ps. 16:11).

But a careful reading of Scripture will show us that, while wonderful and full of joy, Heaven is not yet that place where there are no more tears, pain, etc. These martyrs are not suffering themselves, but they hurt for their brothers and sisters in Christ who are still under the hand of anti-Christ. They are happy, but not yet fully satisfied. This is the state of the current Heaven--angels, believers, even God Himself. Later on, we will see the angels rejoicing that God is finally taking His Kingdom back and ridding

His universe of evil. All of creation is waiting for that day, including our loved ones in Heaven (Rom. 8:22-25).

We also sometimes confuse the state of our loved ones in Heaven today with what it will be when God creates the New Heaven and New Earth. We talk about them having received their new bodies, but this is not yet the case. Remember that when we die here on earth, our souls and spirits leave our bodies. Those two parts of our being are consciously in God's presence at that time, but the resurrection of our bodies does not occur until Jesus returns at the rapture (1 Thess. 4:13-18). We will look at what I call "the history of Heaven" in one of our last flashbacks.

For now, let's flash back to what Scripture shows us about the darkest, most horrible period that will ever occur here on earth—the time that these martyrs were begging God to bring to an end. Let's see what Scripture tells us about what Jesus called "the Great Tribulation."

FLASHBACK 3

The Great Tribulation

Read Daniel 12; 2 Thess. 2:1-10; Matt. 24:15-22; Daniel 9:27; Rev. 12:7-12

Some events from history are painful to recall. Herod's slaughter of babies and toddlers in Bethlehem (Matt. 2). The live human sacrifices of the Incas and Aztecs. The racially justified enslavement of Africans in early American history. The horrific murder of millions of Jews and others by the Nazis during World War 2. The starvation of millions under Stalin and Mao. Mankind's capacity for cruelty and violence has been a widespread problem since before the flood (Gen. 6:11), and every nation and race have participated.

But the worst is yet to come.

An angel told Daniel that just before the time of the resurrection, the worst persecution in the history of Israel will occur (Dan. 12:1). Remember that Hitler's Germany killed more than six million Jews. But that will not be the worst persecution that God's people will have to endure. Jesus told His disciples that this time will be the most horrific and violent in all of history (Matt. 24:21), so completely terrible that God will have to intervene on behalf of His people in order to keep them from being wiped out (Matt. 24:22). This will be possible because hearts will be very hard and love will be rare (Matt. 24:12). What else do we learn about this terrible time from these passages?

First, we know exactly when it will start--at least in relation to the end of this age of earth's history. Halfway through

Daniel's 70th Week, anti-Christ will change from a smooth deceiver to a violent murderer (Dan. 9:27; Daniel 12:7, 11). Scripture states repeatedly that this period will last 3 1/2 years (sometimes counted in years, sometimes in months or days, and sometimes simply stated as **a time, times, and half a time**--but all adding up to exactly half of Daniel's 70th Week). We will look at the specific event on earth that will bring this change about in a later study.

Second, it will begin suddenly. Jesus warns those who are in Jerusalem to not even stop to grab a coat when it happens, but to run away as fast as they can (Matt. 24:16-20). Apparently anti-Christ will be in Jerusalem, where he has before appeared as a friend and ally (Dan. 9:27). But he will suddenly turn on Israel and set up an idol of himself in the temple, demanding to be worshipped (Daniel 9:27; Matt. 24:15). It seems there will be no warning, but a sudden and deadly change.

Third, it will happen only when Israel's protector has been removed. Paul tells believers in Thessalonica that anti-Christ cannot fully reveal himself until the one currently restraining him has been removed (2 Thess. 2:6-8). Some have claimed that this is the Holy Spirit, but nowhere in Scripture are we told that the Holy Spirit will ever be removed from the world. Daniel 12:1, however, tells us that there will come a time when Michael, the archangel who is specifically assigned to protect Israel, **will arise** (Daniel 12:1 NASB). When that happens, the Great Tribulation will begin. This seems clearly to identify Michael as the one holding back the time when evil on earth will do its very worst.

There is one final thing that we learn from the Scriptures about the Great Tribulation. There is an event in Heaven that sets it off. (As promised, we will also learn later about an event on earth that plays an important role.) Scripture tells us that Satan, who no longer lives in Heaven (Luke 10:18), still has access to God there (Job 1:6-7; Zechariah 3:1-2) and loves nothing more than to use that access to accuse God's people of sin and to demand that God judge them (Rev. 12:10). But Rev. 12:7-13 tells us that Satan will try one more time to take control of Heaven. He and his demons will lose that battle, and he will then be forever banned from that place. This will make him angry, and since he cannot defeat God, he will do what he knows hurts God the most--he will pour out his fury on Israel and the church. This will be the true motive for anti-Christ's hate-filled violence, and this hatred will result in the worst time in all of history for God's people to endure.

QUESTION 12

*What happens when the sixth
seal is broken?*

Read Rev. 6:12-17; Matt. 24:29-41; Joel 2:31; Joel 3:15-16

When the sixth seal is broken, events begin to happen in the sky that together form a clear sign that the world is indeed coming to an end. These events are prophesied in Revelation, in Matthew, and in Joel, and it seems clear that these prophecies all refer to the same awesome event. Surely something like this could not happen more than once in human history!

Revelation 6 tells us that first a terrible earthquake will occur. This is not the only earthquake mentioned in Revelation, and maybe not even the worst. (Two great earthquakes are described in Rev. 11 alone.) But the events that follow are without equal. The sun will turn completely black and the moon will become the color of blood. Heavenly bodies will begin falling to earth in large numbers, and the sky itself will be split apart as if someone rolled up a giant scroll. Both mountains and islands made up of huge pillars of stone anchored to the earth will be moved out of their places.

It is safe to say that this will get everyone's attention!

Jesus promised the same set of signs in Matt. 24:29. Joel prophesied many of these same things. All of these prophecies are pointing to one particular moment in end times history. But what do these signs mean to communicate to humanity?

Joel tells us that these signs announce the coming of the

Day of the Lord. Scripture is full of references to this great and terrible day. But what is it? It is the day when God finally sets loose His wrath against Satan's rebel kingdom. It is the moment in time when God turns the tide, putting an end to the horrible slaughter of His children during the Great Tribulation and pouring out His judgments--the trumpets and bowls--against the followers of the beast. (Note that the Great Tribulation continues for the full 3 1/2 years, but as we will see in Revelation 7, God protects those who are His among Israel and the church beginning at this point in time. This is how He cuts the Great Tribulation short for His children as Jesus promised in Matt. 24:22.)

Here is a small sampling of Scriptures that refer to this momentous time in history--the final answer to the "How long?" question that God's children have been asking almost from the beginning: Amos 5:18-20; Malachi 4:1-5; Obadiah 1:15; Ezekiel 30:3; 2 Peter 3:10; 1 Cor. 5:5; 1 Thess. 5:2; 2 Thess. 2:2. Please note that the actual wrath of God does not begin until the seventh seal (which contains the seven trumpets and seven bowls) is broken. But these signs from the sixth seal announce that it is time, and even the lost will recognize that God's wrath is about to fall (Rev. 6:16-17).

Jesus detailed one other event that occurs at this time. He returns and raptures the church! Many wonderful Bible teachers have taught that the rapture of the church occurs at the beginning of Daniel's 70th Week, but if that is the case, it seems very difficult to identify what Jesus is telling us here. He says that the signs in the Heavens which announce the coming of God's wrath come just before He appears in the sky. As He appears, His angels will gather believers around the world. 1 Thess. 4:13-18 tells us the same thing--that the trumpet will sound announcing Christ's return and that the dead in Christ will rise and be joined by living believers who will be transformed into their eternal bodies in the air (1 Cor. 15:51-57)! But if this is the case, why have so many taught that believers will be raptured several years earlier?

One reason is that the Bible promises believers that we will not have to endure God's wrath (1 Thess. 1:10; 5:9). Since these teachers believe the entire final seven years of earth's history is part of God's wrath, they argue that we must be raptured before this time period begins. But as we have just seen, the time of God's wrath (the Day of the Lord) begins after the events in the sky that happen when the sixth seal is broken. Thus believers *can* be on earth during Daniel's 70th Week, including part of the last half of that week which is the Great Tribulation.

This is unsettling news to many who have been taught that believers will escape this terrible time of persecution. Unfortunately, sometimes God has to stir us up a bit in order to be sure that we are prepared for what is going to happen. Jesus clearly indicated the general time frame of His return in Matthew 24-- although not the day or the hour, as He said those are known only to the Father—will be sometime *after* the beginning of the Great Tribulation which starts halfway through the last seven years of our history.

Let's look a little more closely at the timeline of the end times in our next Flashback.

FLASHBACK 4

The 70 Weeks Prophecy

Read Daniel 9:24-27

"Seventy weeks have been decreed for your people and your holy city, to finish the transgression, to make an end of sin, to make atonement for iniquity, to bring in everlasting righteousness, to seal up vision and prophecy and to anoint the most holy place. 25 "So you are to know and discern that from the issuing of a decree to restore and rebuild Jerusalem until Messiah the Prince there will be seven weeks and sixty-two * weeks; it will be built again, with plaza and moat, even in times of distress. 26 "Then after the sixty-two * weeks the Messiah will be cut off and have nothing, and the people of the prince who is to come will destroy the city and the sanctuary. And its end will come with a flood; even to the end there will be war; desolations are determined. 27 "And he will make a firm covenant with the many for one week, but in the middle of the week he will put a stop to sacrifice and grain offering; and on the wing of abominations will come one who makes desolate, even until a complete destruction, one that is decreed, is poured out on the one who makes desolate." (NASB)

This has been a confusing and controversial prophecy for some, but a careful reading in the context of other end times prophecies leads us to a clear conclusion. In Daniel 9, Daniel has discovered prophecies given to Jeremiah that show that God would rescue Israel from their captivity in Babylon after 70 years had passed. Daniel knew that that time was near, so he began to pray, first for God to forgive the sins that had brought Israel into captivity, and then that He would graciously restore the nation to its homeland. In response to his prayer, God sent Gabriel to give him an overview of His plan for Israel for the remainder of history!

Gabriel tells Daniel that God has set aside **seventy weeks** (literally **seventy sevens** in the original language) for his people. This is the usual designation for a week, a period of seven days. The word itself, however, does not apply only to days, but to any group of seven things or time periods. In this case, we know from having seen most of this prophecy fulfilled, that it applies not to groups of seven days but to sets of seven years. God is telling Daniel that, over a 490 year period (seventy times seven), He will finish His work to bring Israel out of sin and to Himself. Here are the purposes stated for this 490 year time period in vs. 24:

...to finish the transgression, to make an end of sin, to make atonement for iniquity, to bring in everlasting righteousness, to seal up vision and prophecy and to anoint the most holy place. (Daniel 9:24 NASB)

Israel's entire history, since God called Abraham to be the father of the nation, has been one of repeated cycles of sin, God's redemption, then falling back again into sin. The New Testament tells us that this is because human beings have a sin nature and cannot in their own power make themselves righteous (Gal. 3:1-14; 21-29). Jesus' sacrifice on the cross made it possible for our sins to be forgiven and for us to be changed from the inside out through a lifelong process known as sanctification, which is the process of being made holy (Romans 6:19). While the church began with the Jews, the majority in Israel rejected the Gospel message and has to this day. Romans 11:26 tells us that a day will come when what is left of Israel (after anti-Christ's murderous rampage) will finally trust Christ. This whole process will be the main outcome of this seventy weeks of years.

Furthermore, God tells Daniel that the first 69 weeks of

years will take place between his day and the crucifixion and resurrection of Christ. The first week of years will begin when a pagan king (Cyrus of Persia) allows the Jews to return home and rebuild their temple. After seven weeks (49 years) have passed, the temple will be finished. Then it will be another 62 weeks of years (434 years) until Messiah comes and completes His work to provide for everyone's redemption—Jew and Gentile alike. (Being "cut off" is the Old Testament term for execution—Gen. 17:14; Ex. 31:14.) We know from history that this is exactly how these first 69 weeks actually played out. Then in 70 A.D. the Romans, to put down a Jewish revolt, came in and destroyed Jerusalem and the temple, completing the prophecy up through vs. 26.

Vs. 27 then describes the events of the last of the 70 sets of seven years (which will most often be called "Daniel's 70th Week" in this study). Like the very first week of years, Daniel's 70th Week will begin with an agreement between Israel and the most powerful leader in the Gentile world. He is called here **the prince who is to come** (Daniel 9:26 NASB), and it is noted that he comes from the same nation that would destroy the temple in 70 A.D., which we now know was the Roman Empire. This peace agreement will last for half of Daniel's 70th Week. Then suddenly, in the middle of the week, this prince will break the covenant with Israel, will defile their temple and set up an image of himself to be worshiped there, and will begin killing Jews (and Christians) at an alarming rate. But God promises Daniel that He will bring an end to this terrible prince and his reign of terror.

Sometimes in the New Testament we will read about a **mystery** that God has revealed. This is usually something that He did not clearly tell Israel before Christ came, but later revealed to the church (Rom. 11:25; Col 1:25-28). The church itself is one such mystery, and the church age is what is not revealed here to Daniel. To read the text, we would not know that there would be any interruption in the 490 years that God reveals to Daniel. But God did not tell Daniel, who was primarily concerned with his own nation, about the period during which Gentiles would be the majority among the redeemed—the church age. He was instead focusing on what He would do to provide for Israel's redemption in Christ and when Israel as a whole would finally come to Christ. Those two events are separated by 2,000 years and counting.

This prophecy, fulfilled exactly as God promised through the first coming of Christ, awaits only the last seven years of this age of Earths history! And that is exactly the time period that we are covering with this study. When will it happen? The Bible does not tell us that—but it does give us signs for which we can watch.

Are we being watchful or wasteful of the time that God has given us? Our job in the meantime, of course, is to share Jesus so that all who are willing will be prepared! Is that the priority of your life today? If not, how can you make it to be so? We dare not get lulled to sleep by all the time that has passed, for the time is indeed short, and these events will seem very sudden when they actually happen. Be prepared!

QUESTION 13

What does God stop everything to do?

Read Rev. 7:1-8

There are two very important things that must be done before God will allow His judgments to fall. (Remember that the Day of the Lord judgments begin with the opening of the seventh seal.) There are two groups of people whom God wants to protect from these judgments. We know that He protects the church/ true believers with the rapture, and we will see the results of that event in the next study. But there is another group that is very special to Him that He will protect in a different way.

Remember where we are in the progress of the seals/Daniel's 70th Week. A world suffering under the violent anger of anti-Christ has been shaken by an earthquake strong enough to move mountains and islands. The sun has gone dark and the moon has turned the color of blood. Showers of heavenly bodies have crashed to the ground. The sky has opened up, splitting apart as if someone has suddenly closed a scroll. And Jesus has appeared in the sky.

The beast's followers recognize that He has come to execute God's wrath, and they try to hide between rocks and in caves. As they cower, Christ commands that the believing dead arise and sends His angels to rapture believers, who are given their eternal bodies even as they rise to join the resurrected dead. The Bible does not tell us exactly where the Lord goes from that point, but I believe that He goes to the group of people that we are about to discuss in order to introduce them as a people and as individuals to their Messiah (Rev. 14:1).

As if what has already gone on in the sky is not enough, four very special angels are dispatched to hold back all of the world's winds. Imagine standing outside and feeling absolutely no stirring of the air around you. These angels are identified as the four angels who have been granted permission to **harm...earth...sea** and **trees**. This almost certainly refers to the angels who sound the first four trumpets, as this is the result of their work (Rev. 8:6-12) and they begin their work with the opening of the seventh seal which is soon to come.

Another angel rises from the east and commands them to wait until he has sealed a group of God's special servants. Like the servants of the beast, they are sealed on their foreheads but presumably with God's name, indicating that they belong to Him. The sealed are 12 groups of 12,000 people from 12 tribes of the sons of Israel.

Interestingly, Dan is not mentioned among those who are sealed, although there is an allotment for Dan in the Millennial Kingdom (Ezekiel 48:1-2). While we do not know why Dan is left out—possibly because there are not enough from that tribe left to seal 12,000—we do know that these are not the only Jews who will be protected from God's judgments. Rev. 14:4 tells us that they are **firstfruits**, indicating that there are more to follow. So while for whatever reason Dan is not included in this group, his tribe will be represented when Christ reigns in the promised Kingdom. In Dan's absence, the sons of Joseph (Ephraim and Manasseh) are each represented by 12,000 sealed men. Ephraim and Manasseh received a similar honor when the land was allotted under Joshua, since the Levites did not receive their own allotment of land.

It seems clear that these 12 groups of 12,000 will be the leaders of Israel during the time of God's judgments and into the Millennial Kingdom. They will be some of the most important mortals on earth during a time when mortals and resurrected believers are present together! And they are the beginning of what God has long promised but His chosen people have resisted—the coming of Israel to faith in Christ. These will be special men indeed, and the first fulfillment of a promise for all of those who have prayed for Jerusalem's peace (Ps. 122:6)!

QUESTION 14

Who are these people in Heaven?

Read Rev. 7:9-17; 1 Thess. 4:13-18; John 12:12-13

Before John's eyes, a huge multitude of people suddenly appears in Heaven before God's throne. John cannot count them. They come from every conceivable nation, ethnic group, and language group. And they are wearing white robes and holding palm branches.

Do you remember Jesus' "triumphal" entry into Jerusalem? That moment was the fulfillment of a prophecy recorded in Zechariah 9:9-- **Rejoice greatly, O daughter of Zion! Shout in triumph, O daughter of Jerusalem! Behold, your king is coming to you; He is just and endowed with salvation, Humble, and mounted on a donkey, Even on a colt, the foal of a donkey.** (NASB)

At that time, He was met by adoring crowds waving palm branches. They proclaimed Him King and shouted "Hosanna," which means, "Save us, we pray!" Palm branches had been a symbol of victory since they had been carried into Jerusalem to celebrate the Maccabees' victory over the Syrians. None understood that day that He was coming to save us not by overthrowing Rome, but by dying on a cross. But these people in Heaven now waving palm branches know full well the cost of their salvation and are worshiping Father and Son from grateful hearts!

An elder then asks John the same question that we are asking: "Who are these people?" John does not know, but the elder kindly tells him that they are the ones who have come out of the Great Tribulation. This means that they are saved human beings, which is also indicated by their white robes washed clean by the Lamb's blood.

Now we come to the key part of the question. It is tempting to see these as only believers who will be killed during the Great Tribulation. That would be the simplest explanation. But if we take the surrounding events into account, I think we will come to a different conclusion. I believe that these are all believers, Old and New Testament believers, who lived up to the time of the rapture. Remember that the rapture will occur as Jesus appears in the sky right after the dramatic signs that appear in the Heavens. Since this vision directly follows the opening of the sixth seal (which includes the rapture), it makes sense that these are the resurrected believers of all of history, which would also help to explain the huge numbers as well as the ethnic diversity.

But how can all believers of all time be said to come out of the Great Tribulation? Remember that 1 Thessalonians 4:13-18 tells us that when the trumpet sounds and Jesus appears, the dead in Christ will all rise and then be joined by living believers who will be transformed in the air into their eternal bodies. This happens during the Great Tribulation; therefore, all of these people, even if they died before the Great Tribulation, will literally come out of it in their resurrected bodies and into Heaven where they will be blessed and comforted forever!

This is the time when they will be relieved of all earthly cares—hunger, heat, etc. And this is the time when all tears will come to an end, as all believers have been rescued, believing Jews protected and sealed, and now judgment has come on the rebel kingdom of anti-Christ. Best of all, God will personally welcome them into His presence and provide a home for them—something which many persecuted believers throughout the centuries have been denied. But it is the intimate, face-to-face presence of God Himself—begged for but denied to Moses and so many others while on earth—that will make this time so sweet. And Moses and all of those others who asked for this will be among this group now receiving the answer to their prayer in full!

Raptured believers will then be able to focus on God while He takes care of all of the enemies on earth. "How long?" has now been answered. Soon all will be well with the universe once again —and forever!

QUESTION 15

*What happens when the sev-
enth seal is broken?*

Read Rev. 8:1-6

What happens when the seventh seal is broken? Nothing. At least not for half an hour. Seems odd, doesn't it? Whenever any of the first six seals was broken, action began immediately. Big, sweeping, sometimes terrible events burst onto the scene. But now, nothing. In fact, Heaven, where angels proclaim God's holiness without pause, suddenly falls silent.

As Gandalf might say, this is the "deep breath before the plunge," the moment for which all of the saints and all of Heaven have been waiting has finally arrived. It deserves a few moments of silence before the fireworks begin.

And when it is over, literal fireworks begin! As the seven angels prepare to blow the seven trumpets and to let loose their judgments, another angel gathers all of the incense from the altar, along with all of the prayers of all of the saints of all time—all of the "How longs?" of history. He lights the incense with fire from the altar and hurls it to earth, causing massive peals of thunder, bolts of lightning, and another earthquake. The prayers of God's people are literally incorporated into the fire of judgment that God sends down on anti-Christ's perverted kingdom!

This is as powerful a picture as we find in all of Scripture about prayer. Sometimes we are frustrated when it seems that God takes forever to answer our prayers, just as believers have been frustrated by the slowness of God's judgment against the evil in this world. But this passage reminds us that God will never forget our faithful petitions. And, when the time is right, He will answer, often in more awesome and dramatic fashion than we could ever have imagined. God loves His people and never forgets them. In fact, His delays are usually for their benefit.

The Lord is not slow about His promise, as some count slowness, but is patient toward you, not wishing for any to perish but for all to come to repentance. (2 Peter 3:9 NASB)

QUESTION 16

What happens when the first four trumpets are blown?

Read Rev. 8:7-12

The blowing of the first four trumpets brings massive judgments against all of the basic elements of life on earth. Just as the plagues on Egypt were actually judgments against the false gods that they credited with providing for their existence, so these judgments prove to human beings that the things they think they can count on to be immovable and eternal here on earth are actually not either of those things.

The first four trumpets destroy one third of all vegetation on earth, one third of both fresh and salt water life, and one third of the light provided by the heavenly bodies, which had apparently been restored to their original state after they were used for signs announcing the coming of God's wrath. Such a display would literally shake the foundations of things that people living under anti-Christ's reign would assume would always be there for their support and for their enjoyment. It will also prove that neither anti-Christ nor the dragon is really God since they are powerless to stop what He is doing.

Perhaps a better question at this point is: why only destroy one third of everything? Why not completely destroy all of these things and be done with it? The most likely explanation, knowing God's character as we do from Scripture, is that He is still at this point offering those who have not taken the mark of the beast an opportunity to repent and believe. God is always slow to anger and slow to destroy; He much prefers mercy and salvation. And while the beast has been busy putting his mark on many who are not believers, it is almost certain that he will not be able to get to everyone on earth before Jesus returns to frustrate his plans. And we will see a little later that it is necessary that some will still be left unmarked and so still have the opportunity to repent and believe in Jesus.

QUESTION 17

What is a "woe"?

Read Rev. 8:13; Numbers 21:29; 1 Samuel 4:7; Is. 3:9; Matt. 11:21; Matt. 18:7

After the first four angels have sounded their trumpets, an eagle flies into view pronouncing woes upon those living on earth because of the next three trumpets. He repeats the word "woe" three times, indicating that each of the next three trumpets is actually a "woe." But what does that word mean?

"Woe" is a little word that packs a powerful punch. It is a word of dire warning, and throughout Scripture it is a word promising terrible and final judgments from the hand of God. The scriptures that you have read are just a small sample of the Bible's proclamations of woe, but in each case they tell of powerful judgments for terrible sins.

In Numbers, God pronounces woes upon Moab because they refused to help the children of Israel on their way to the promised land, trying to curse them through the prophet Balaam instead. In 1 Samuel 4, the Philistines recognized woe coming to them as the Ark of the Covenant was brought into the camp of Israel. They ended up defeating Israel and capturing the Ark, but the Ark brought dire woes upon them and their false gods, causing them to send it back in desperation. Isaiah warns of woes to come upon God's people who no longer even try to hide their sins but celebrate them like Sodom did. And Jesus warned both the cities that had seen His miracles but refused to believe and those who would cause little ones to stumble that woeful judgments awaited them.

In each case, these were not simply light warnings, but were final promises that God had reached the end of His patience and that their sins had become so serious that He could no longer show mercy and look away. This is also the case here. Anti-Christ's rebel kingdom has reached its end, and these last three trumpet judgments (the last of which includes the rapid and final bowl judgments) will complete the process of setting things right once again.

All of Scripture's messages of judgment are meant to be warnings. A time will come when it is too late for mercy. God longs for us to repent and believe (2 Peter 3:9), but will not withhold His hand of justice forever. The right time to repent and believe is always right now (2 Cor. 6:2), because a time will come—and come suddenly--when there will be no more opportunities.

QUESTION 18

Who opens the door to the
bottomless pit/abyss?

Read Rev. 9:1; Rev. 12:4; Luke 10:18

When an angel blows the fifth trumpet, the first woe falls. The event that happens should clue us in to how incredibly terrible this judgment will be. Someone is given a key to open the **bottomless pit** (Rev. 9:1 NASB). We will talk in more detail about the bottomless pit in our next flashback; as we will see, its inhabitants are fearsome and wicked creatures. But who is it that is allowed to set those creatures free?

There are two clues in this verse that I believe identify this being. First, he is called **a star from heaven** (NASB). In Revelation stars are used to describe believers (the church leaders of Chapter 1 and Jacob's sons in Chapter 12), but they also symbolize angelic beings (Rev. 12:4). This includes demons, who are angels who have rebelled against God and no longer serve Him. Since Heaven is where this star came from, it seems clear that this must be an angelic or demonic being.

The star is said to have **fallen to the earth** at some point in the past (**had fallen**), which would indicate that this is a demonic being, since his descent was not voluntary. Satan (as the dragon) is said in Rev. 12:4 to have swept 1/3 of Heaven's angels to earth with his tail. In Luke 10:18, Jesus recounts to His disciples being an eyewitness of Satan himself falling rapidly to the earth, shooting from the heavens like lightning. And, as we will see in

Chapter 12, Satan will fall from Heaven one final time before the Great Tribulation begins. These clues together indicate to me that the one given the key is certainly a demon and seems likely to be Satan himself.

The fact that the key has to be given to him reminds us of something very important. While Satan is the leader of demons, and while they are allowed to do a great deal of evil here on earth, they are not able to do everything that they would like to do. God has at many points in history checked the power of evil —with the flood, at Babel, and in many other smaller ways. No matter how much he might like to do so, Satan cannot set his evil forces free to do all the damage that they would love to do unless God allows it. While I believe He allows us a great deal of freedom to do our worst if we so choose, God reserves the right to limit our freedom at any time, and often does so. Evil is powerful, but still no match for our good and merciful God!

FLASHBACK 5

Imprisoned Angels

Read Jude 1:6; 2 Peter 2:4; Luke 8:30-31; Matt. 8:29; Rev. 9:2-21

We never get a complete explanation anywhere in Scripture, but at some point in time some of the fallen angels were imprisoned by God. Jude tells us that they **did not keep their own domain**—they pushed beyond the boundaries that God had set for them. Jude also tells us that they are bound until **the judgment of the great day**. Since terms like **the great day** refer to the Day of the Lord (the time of His wrath and judgment), it seems clear that the creatures who appear in Rev. 9:2-18 are these imprisoned angels, finally set free to do much that they would have done had God not locked them up.

The demons that Jesus encountered when He freed the Gadarene demoniacs clearly understood what had happened to these fallen angels. Luke mentions that they begged not to be sent into the abyss, and Matthew adds that they asked if Jesus was there to **torment us before the time**. This indicates that these demons understood that they will eventually be cast into the Lake of Fire, but they also knew that God had agreed to allow them freedom until that time. Perhaps they feared that, like the demons mentioned by Jude, they had overstepped the boundaries that God had set for them by possessing these men.

Was there one specific event that caused these demons to be imprisoned, or did different groups do things to be sent to the bottomless pit/abyss at different times? Again, Scripture does not clearly tell us this. There is one event, however, that may explain why at least some of them were there. 1 Peter 19:20 mentions that after His death Jesus went and spoke to imprisoned spirits who had been disobedient before the flood. These certainly could be the spirits of human beings, since, as we have seen, our spirits leave our bodies after we die. But angels are also referred to as spirits in Scripture (Heb. 1:14), so this could be Peter's meaning.

Why is the time before the flood significant? Genesis 6:2 tells us that before the flood **the sons of God** lusted after **the daughters of men**. Some believe this refers to the Godly people of Seth's line intermarrying with the rebellious line of Cain. Others believe, especially since just a bit later the appearance of giants is mentioned, that there were actually demons who inhabited men's bodies in order to cohabitate with human women, somehow enhancing them genetically. We cannot know for certain if the latter is the case (or if it is even possible), but if it is, this would be at least one explanation for why some of these demons have been locked up awaiting the day of God's wrath.

The creatures that appear as the fifth and sixth trumpets sound (the first two woes) have been explained in many ways by Bible students. Some have tried to imagine that John was seeing weapons of modern warfare and trying to explain them. But I believe that because both sets of creatures are connected with imprisoned demons that these also must be demonic creatures themselves.

If this is true, it tells us something very important about Satan. Satan is all about hate. He tries to convince us that he is leading us to rebel against God for our good—that God is keeping us from something good with His laws and commands. But this is just another one of his lies, which Jesus said come so naturally to him (John 8:44). This passage bears that out. Here is Satan releasing demons to attack people on earth. Who are these people? The vast majority are people who have sworn allegiance to his rebel kingdom! They are those who have taken his mark and worshiped him! The church has been raptured. The saved remnant of Israel is being hidden and protected in the wilderness. So Satan is now pouring out his wrath on His own followers. How pure is his hatred of people created and loved by God!

And here is perhaps the most chilling part. Even after these demons wreak havoc on them for months (Rev. 9:10), those loyal to the beast still refuse to repent! They will neither give up their idols nor their immoralities and violence. People say all the time that if they could just see God or some proof of the supernatural that they would believe. Most of those who saw Jesus' miracles eventually cried out to have Him crucified. And here men have seen Jesus appear in the sky, have seen believers disappear, have seen demons visibly unleashed upon them—and they still refuse to repent of their sins and put their faith in Jesus.

One other thing becomes clear as we put these passages of Scripture together. Cartoons and popular theology often have Satan and his demons ruling over Hell, prodding the poor sufferers there with pitchforks and tormenting them at every turn. But this is not the picture that we are given in Scripture. Most demons are not yet in Hell, and none of them want to be there. They will not be the tormentors, but will be the most terribly tormented of all. God rules in Heaven, and He also rules Hell. The demons dread the day when they will be sent there, although they know that that day is coming.

QUESTION 19

Who is this strong angel and what is
the little book that he gives to John?

Read Rev. 10:1-11

There are different orders of angels. Michael is in Scripture called an archangel (Jude 1:9), the strongest of God's angels. Like people, God apparently gave angels different gifts and different levels of ability. And, like people, God no doubt expects them to be faithful with their gifts and obedient to His will.

Some have speculated that this angel is actually Christ, since the descriptions of his face and feet seem to match those of the glorified Lord Jesus in Revelation 1. But he is called **another strong angel**, which indicates that he is on the same level as the angels who are assigned to blow the seven trumpets. This makes him a high-ranking angel, but still only an angel and not our Lord. It seems likely that all beings in Heaven who live in the presence of God and His Shekinah glory (as described by John in Rev. 4) reflect His glory and holiness and pure light. The rainbow on his head is clearly a reflection of God's multi-faceted, multi-colored glory as described by John.

This angel has a special message for John. God tends to use high-ranking angels to deliver very important messages to human beings. (One example is Gabriel, who appeared both to Daniel and to Mary.) This angel carries a small open book, and he takes his stand with one foot on the land and one on the sea as he speaks to John.

Why did he stand like this? No doubt to declare God's sovereignty over land and sea, over every nation and people. (The Gentile nations are often represented by the sea as we will see in Chapter 13.) It could also be a direct statement promising that God will conquer the two coming beasts, members of Satan's mock trinity, one of whom comes from the sea and one from the land. His cry seems to have been a cry of victory for God and for His Kingdom.

The seven peals of thunder responded to his cry, but John was commanded not to write what they said. Some end times events remain a mystery until the events actually happen. He declared to John that the seventh angel who was about to sound would bring God's final judgments to the world without further delay. Then the voice from Heaven gave John a curious command —to eat the little book that the angel was holding.

John ate the book just as he was commanded to do and immediately experienced what he was told that he would experience—a sweet taste but an upset stomach. We will discuss this in a moment in our next flashback about the nature of prophecy. But after he had eaten the book, he was commanded to prophecy again about what was soon to come upon the world.

Once again we find ourselves asking about the contents of a book or scroll. I believe that the two are actually related. The first scroll that only the Lamb could open is, I believe, the record of the events that Revelation promises will take place at the end-- events which will happen when the seals are opened, the trumpets are blown, and the bowls are poured out over the earth. But the next three chapters of Revelation interrupt this sequence somewhat, giving us more information about the two witnesses (Chapter 11), the dragon and Israel (Chapter 12), and the beast and false prophet (Chapter 13). John is told that he is to prophesy **concerning many peoples and nations and tongues and kings**, and this is exactly what happens in those chapters. I believe that this little book is something of a supplemental prophecy to the main message of Revelation contained in the scroll. It fills in some of the gaps and details concerning some of the important figures of

Daniel's 70th Week while momentarily interrupting the description of the events that will happen during that time.

FLASHBACK 6

The Nature of Prophecy

Read Rev. 10:9-11; Numbers 12:6-8; Deut. 13:1-5; Deut. 18:18-22; 1 Kings 18:22; 1 Chron. 17:1-4; Luke 4:17-21/Isaiah 61:1-6; Isaiah 9:6-7; Mal. 4:5/Matt. 17:10-13/Matt. 11:14

Prophecy is one of the most intense of all of the spiritual gifts, and the prophet's job is one of the most difficult. God does not tell us everything that is going to happen for a reason; we would not be able to bear knowing everything that will happen in our lives. But prophets often have to bear the burden of knowing difficult things that lie ahead for them and for those they love. In fact, the prophetic message is often called a "burden" (translated as **oracle** in the NASB—Is. 13:1; Nahum 1:1; Habakkuk 1:1). It was not easy to be God's chosen messenger to His people.

John experienced this physically in Rev. 10. He was commanded to eat the small book, and when he did, although it was sweet to taste, it resulted in an upset stomach. This is the difficult burden of every prophet, carrying and sharing God's revelation. It is sometimes difficult to share because it carries bad news to people the prophet loves. Other times the prophet faces opposition from those who do not like the message. Powerful people often persecuted God's prophets. And the life of the prophet is lonely, since people are afraid to associate with one who is so close to a holy God (1 Kings 18:22). The prophet must speak, however, or, as Jeremiah described it, feel as if his insides are on fire (Jer. 20:9).

Another reason that the life of the prophet is so hard is that he is held to an incredibly high standard. God often warned His people about false prophets, and gave standards in Deuteronomy 13 and 18 which helped them to distinguish between men He had called and men who were speaking on their own initiative. There were two basic standards. First, any time that a man said that God had given him a message, he had to be right. If he predicted a future event and it did not happen—even just once--then he was to be dismissed as a false prophet.

Second, even if he seemed to perform some sort of miracle, his listeners still had to compare what he asked them to do to God's already revealed Word. For example, if someone who claimed to be a prophet performed an impressive sign, then told the people to go worship idols, the people were to ignore the sign and reject this prophet. And any time a prophet claimed to speak for God and was wrong, the penalty was death.

As if these things were not enough to complicate the prophet's life, the prophetic messages themselves were usually difficult to understand. Peter tells us in 1 Peter 1:10-12 that we have received knowledge about God's plan for our salvation that the Old Testament prophets begged to understand but could not. He says that we have been shown things that even angels would like to see. God told Moses and his siblings that His habit of speaking aloud to Moses was not His usual form of communication with His prophets. He said that He normally used dreams and visions and **dark sayings** (Num. 12:8 NASB). So prophets were often given prophecies that even they did not fully understand. This was especially true when the prophecies had multiple fulfillments.

We will encounter this aspect of prophecy as we move forward with our studies in Revelation. Two examples that were included in the reading for this flashback will hopefully help us to understand this concept a little more clearly. In Luke 4, Jesus read part of a prophecy about Himself from Isaiah 61. The entire prophecy applies to Him, so why did He stop? He stopped because part of the prophecy described what He would do when He came the first time. The rest of the prophecy concerned His second coming. This is one reason why we should not be too hard on the people of Israel for expecting Jesus to bring the Kingdom at His first advent. Many of the prophecies concerning His two comings speak of both at the same time.

Another example that connects closely with our end times study is the Old Testament prophecy concerning the coming of Elijah in advance of the Day of the Lord. Jesus clearly told His disciples that John the Baptist was a fulfillment of that prophecy (having come not as a reincarnation of Elijah but in **the spirit and power** (Luke 1:17 NASB) of that prophet). He also said, however that Elijah was still to come (Matt. 17:11), meaning that the prophecy has more than one fulfillment. Just as Jesus' coming was divided into two separate appearances which serve different purposes (the first for salvation, the second to bring judgment and the Kingdom), so Elijah's return would be two-fold.

As we can see, the life of a prophet was not an easy one. He often had to confront powerful people or deliver a message that his friends and neighbors were not eager to hear. Sometimes he must have seemed crazy to them (Ezekiel 4:1-8; Isaiah 20:1-5). People were afraid of him because of His connection with God the Father. And the message itself was a terrible burden that he could not hold inside; perhaps worse, it was often confusing and hard to understand. John's duty in relaying Revelation to us was no less intense. We need to be thankful for faithful prophets who speak God's words to us despite all of the hardships involved.

QUESTION 20

Why does God have John measure the temple area?

Read Rev. 11:1-2; Zech. 2:1-4; Psalm 108:5-8; Ezekiel 45:3

Measuring in Scripture sets limits. Those limits may be the border of territory for the various tribes or for a nation. They may be setting aside a place and the people in it for a certain purpose. Ps. 108:5-8 has God measuring Israel so as to set that territory aside and declaring the people there His own. God has Ezekiel measure his vision of the Millennial temple, Millennial Jerusalem, and the territory of the nation of Israel for that future time (Ez. 45-48). In Zechariah 2, the prophet encounters a man going out to measure Jerusalem, and God uses that as an opportunity to prophecy through Zechariah about the wide-open city during the Millennial Kingdom, its borders personally protected by Him!

In Revelation 11, God has John measure the future Jerusalem as it will exist during Daniel's 70th Week. He is told to measure the temple and altar with the worshipers who are there, but to leave out the outer court (the Court of the Gentiles), because He will allow the forces of anti-Christ to dominate that area for 3 ½ years. This speaks to the domination of Jerusalem by anti-Christ during the Great Tribulation, but reminds John that there will be a faithful, believing remnant of Israel that will survive and be protected by God during that time.

The Millennial Kingdom will reverse this, exalting and expanding Jerusalem and making it the most important city on earth. Gentiles will pour into it not to conquer, but to learn and to meet her King—King Jesus! This is no doubt a reminder to John during his time of persecution that God will protect and one day exalt His children. Even during our darkest times here on earth, there is hope for our future!

QUESTION 21

Who are these two witnesses?

Read Rev. 11:3-6; Zechariah 4; 1 Kings 17:1; 2 Kings 1:10; Ex. 7-11

God tells John that during the time that the Gentiles dominate the outer court of the temple—the time of the Great Tribulation, the last half of Daniel's 70th Week—He will place two very irritating flies right in anti-Christ's back door. These two witnesses, who bear the characteristics and powers of two very prominent Old Testament prophets, will preach the truth during the Great Tribulation; for most of that time, anti-Christ will be powerless to stop them!

The two prophets prophecy for 3 ½ years, possibly beginning a short time before the Great Tribulation begins. They will wear sackcloth, a rough cloth often worn to demonstrate repentance before God. They are the fulfillment of Zechariah's prophecy in Zech. 4—actually, the second fulfillment of that prophecy.

When the prophecy was given, it applied to the political leader (Zerubbabel, descendant of David) and the religious leader (Joshua the high priest) of that day after the return from Babylon. But the prophecy also had a far fulfillment in these two witnesses at the very end of earth's history. That prophecy emphasized the empowerment of the Holy Spirit (symbolized as He often is in Scripture by olive oil, with which prophets, priests, and kings were anointed) Who would grant success to Joshua and Zerubbabel, as well as to these two end-times preachers.

The witnesses are also reminiscent of the two most prominent prophets of Israel's history—Elijah and Moses. Moses was the lawgiver, leading Israel out of Egyptian captivity. Elijah was one of the most powerful prophets of the later kingdom period. Their ministries foreshadow the ministry of these two witnesses. They have the powers of both men—to stop rainfall on earth and to call down fire on their enemies (Elijah) and to send plagues on anti-Christ's kingdom (Moses). This is, I believe the final fulfillment of the prophecy of one who is to come in the spirit and power of Elijah as promised by Jesus (Matt. 17:11). During the time of their ministry no one, including anti-Christ, will be able to harm them.

QUESTION 22

What happens to these witnesses?

Read Rev. 11:7-14

God protects His witnesses until they have completed their work. When they are done, He allows them to be killed—but even this decision has a very important purpose. The curious part of this passage is this: who is it exactly who kills them?

Here is the exact description from Scripture:

...the beast that comes up out of the abyss will make war with them, and overcome them and kill them. (Rev. 11:7 NASB)

This is an interesting description, and appears to be a combination of two important end-times figures. Chapter 13 will introduce us to two *beasts*, one who rises out of the sea, and one who rises from the earth. We have already read about a captain of the demons who are currently bound in the *abyss*—known in Rev. 9 as the destroyer (Rev. 9:11). But do you notice the problem? Neither of the beasts are identified as coming out of the abyss.

Is it even possible to identify the murderer of these two powerful witnesses? I believe that it is, and we will fill in the details in the following chapters. For now, let's leave it at this: there may be a time when the destroyer and one of the beasts become one! We will see how this is accomplished in a future study.

The response to the murder of these two witnesses in the streets of Jerusalem (vs. 8; Luke 13:33) is telling. The whole world, witnessing their deaths, has a celebration on par with our modern-day Christmas! They will be so glad to be rid of these two men who have laid their lost souls bare by continuously preaching God's truth that they will do them the supreme dishonor of not allowing their bodies to be buried.

For three and one-half days they will celebrate the beast's great victory—until suddenly God resurrects them and calls them up to Heaven. When this happens, He also strikes Jerusalem with a terrible earthquake that destroys $1/10^{th}$ of the city and kills 7,000 people. Unlike the judgments that have fallen before, this one has a positive spiritual impact. Those in Jerusalem who are not killed finally give glory to the true and living God after witnessing this mighty miracle. Their resurrections actually lead to a change of heart for at least some in a hard-hearted, beast-dominated world.

This bit of good news is quickly followed, however, by the announcement that the final woe—the seventh trumpet judgment—is about to fall. The events that follow, including the seven bowl judgments, must happen in rapid succession during the final few days of the Great Tribulation.

QUESTION 23

*What announcement is made
about God's Kingdom?*

Read Rev. 11:15-19

When the seventh angel sounds, the most important announcement in history is made. It is finally time. God's Kingdom has come!

The reestablishment of God's Kingdom is actually the theme of both the Bible and of history. Sin and evil are all part of the rebellion against God the Creator's rightful rule over our lives. The world as we know it is the result of what happens when we try to rule our own lives. (It is actually not the full result. As we have seen, God's grace has intervened and kept things from getting as bad as they could be.) The Great Tribulation is the most complete revelation of the potential results of sin and rebellion that the world will ever see.

The coming Kingdom is the hope of Israel throughout both testaments. God promised David that a time would come when Israel would no longer be threatened and when his direct descendant would rule his Kingdom forever (2 Samuel 7:8-16). From this time on Israel looked forward to the fulfillment of that promise, and their longing became even more intense after their return from captivity in Babylon. The prophets spoke again and again of the coming Kingdom which we know now as the Millennial Kingdom. Isaiah, Ezekiel, and especially Zechariah comforted Israel with details of what was to come—peace all around (even within the animal kingdom), successful crops and plentiful food, God's personal presence protecting them (removing the need for protective walls around Jerusalem), and an expanded territory and role for Jerusalem, which will become the capital of the world. No wonder the people expected so much from their Messiah!

It is also no wonder that the disciples asked Jesus again and again when this Kingdom would come. Neither group understood at the time that Messiah first had to save His people from their sins and institute the church age—the great age of evangelism and missions—to prepare as many people as would repent and believe to be restored to God's eternal Kingdom.

It is fitting that the elders fall face down to worship and praise God for taking back His Kingdom. As His redeemed children, they have experienced the persecution of the nations in rebellion against God. They have been among those asking, "How long?" They await, along with all the saints, their vindication before a mocking, unbelieving world. And now that time, and their full reward, has arrived.

Believers are often accused of being the ones who are destroying our planet—either its ecosystem or its peace and harmony. King Ahab accused the prophet Elijah of being the **troubler of Israel** (1 Kings 18:17 NASB), even though he and his family were actually the problem, rebelling against Israel's God and serving the Baals. The chorus of false accusations continues today. But the elders speak the truth; it is those who have rebelled against the Creator who have destroyed His creation. His mercy has allowed them ample time to repent and believe in the true King. Now His final judgments will fall.

There is great significance in the opening of the holiest place in Heaven and the revealing of the heavenly ark of the covenant that rests there. The earthly ark, built on the pattern of the heavenly one, was the place where God met personally with His people—but that holy of holies was sealed off with a heavy veil. That was for the protection of the people, sinners who could not survive being in God's direct presence (Exodus 33:15-20). When Christ died, the veil sealing off the holiest place in the earthly temple was torn apart, opening up access to God since now our sins have been paid for in full. We can approach God as sinless beings—not because we have no sin, but because Jesus has taken our sin upon Himself and given us His righteousness in its place!

The opening of the holiest place in the Heavenly temple is no threat to the redeemed who are there; they have already been ushered personally into God's presence and comforted by Him. But removing the barrier to the heavenly holy of holies to the followers of the beast offers no comfort, only judgment. Many of his followers have cried for centuries for God to show Himself. In His mercy, He has not done so, since they were not ready. As the seventh trumpet sounds, mercy is no more. The rest of the unsaved will now have to face God unprepared and hopeless.

FLASHBACK 7

Kingdoms Come

Read Gen. 3:1-8

We cannot truly grasp the full impact of Revelation without understanding at least a bit about the history of the Kingdom of God and its importance to all of us. This would be a study worthy of its own book, but we will try to hit just a few highlights here. I strongly recommend that you search out more Scriptures regarding the Kingdom for a better understanding of this vital subject.

As we saw earlier, God established His Kingship over the universe simply by creating it (Rev. 4:11). It belongs to Him, and He has the right to rule it as He sees fit. We can rejoice that He is a kind and loving ruler who cares about the well-being of His creatures. When Satan tempted Adam and Eve to rebel against their Creator, he did so by lying and convincing them that God really did not have their best interests at heart. Their fall into sin drew the entire creation, which had been put under their authority (Gen. 1:27-28), into the mess that their rebellion had created (Rom. 8:19-22).

Read Rev. 12:3-4; Ezekiel 28:1-18; Is. 14:12-17

Of course, Satan had been the first to rebel against God's rightful reign. As we learn in Rev. 12, he lured 1/3 of Heaven's angels into his rebel kingdom. Two Old Testament kings were compared with him—the King of Tyre (Ezekiel 28) and the King of Babylon (Is. 14). In both cases, the prophecies against them tell them that they will suffer the same fate as this fallen angel because they are both driven by the same motivation—pride, including the desire to be god of their own lives and to command and control others.

Because all human beings have sinned (Rom. 3:23), all human beings are rebels against the rightful King. And our motivation is the same as that of the original rebel—we want to be in control of our own lives instead of serving God and allowing Him to be our Lord. Whether we fully realize it or not, we are like those Old Testament kings, wanting to be our own gods, to be worshiped and served rather than to worship and serve the only worthy Ruler. Those who rise to positions of great power come under even greater temptation to exalt themselves and to demand the adoration and obedience of others. World history is littered with those who, for a little while, rose up to rule many, only to find the same end as the least of their subjects after a few short years of glory.

Read Genesis 10:1-11:9

God created the institution of human government after Noah and his family left the ark (Gen. 9). An increasing penchant for violence that threatened to destroy the human race had led to the judgment of the flood (Gen. 6:11-13). Now God was giving mankind some tools to help to check future violence. It was very important that humanity survive; otherwise the Savior would not be born and all of humanity would be lost forever.

In Genesis 10, we see Noah's descendants begin to develop into families which would eventually become the nations that we encounter in Scripture. Japheth's descendants would include the Medes (**Madai**) and the Greeks (**Javan**). Ham's descendants would include the Canaanites, the Egyptians (**Mizraim**), and the Philistines (**Casluhim**). Shem's children would become the Assyrians (**Asshur**), the Syrians (**Aram**), the Persians (**Elam**), the Babylonians, and a small nation that would become the central focus of the rest of Scripture—the Hebrews (**sons of Eber**).

We also see a pattern of groups trying to settle in desirable areas and to fortify themselves and gain power and glory. Nimrod, for example, settled the fertile area of Shinar which would eventually host the great empires of Assyria and Babylon. He built both of their chief cities—Babel and Nineveh, although his Semitic cousins would be the ones who would bring those kingdoms to greatness.

As He had with Adam's children, God commanded Noah's descendants to have children and to spread out over the earth (Gen. 9:1). There seemed to be a tendency to stop after a certain amount of spreading in order to build something out of pride in defiance of God's command. This happened in a great way at Babel, where the people gathered to build a city and a name for themselves. God intervened in a powerful way by confusing their language, forcing them to divide into groups that could only communicate with one another and to separate into what would become nations. As at the flood, God's intervention at Babel was vital to the survival of the human race and the coming of the Savior.

Read Genesis 11:10-32; Rev. 12; Gen. 37:9-11

Speaking of the coming of the Savior, the last part of Genesis 11 introduces us to a special nation, called out by God Himself, created for the express purpose of bringing a Savior for all the nations. This nation would come from Abraham through his son Isaac and grandson Jacob. Abraham is first introduced to us in Genesis 11.

A dramatic shift takes place beginning with Genesis Chapter 12. Up until this time, the Book of Genesis tells the story of all of Adam's descendants, then all of Noah's. But beginning with Chapter 12, the focus shifts clearly to one developing nation—the nation of Israel. The rest of Scripture focuses almost exclusively on this nation, with other nations being discussed primarily as they interact with (often to oppress) God's people.

A big part of the story of the Old Testament is the battle

between Satan's rebel kingdom and God's chosen nation, represented by the dragon and the woman in Rev. 12. The identity of the woman wearing the sun and stars and standing on the moon is clearly understood when we look at Joseph's dream in Gen. 37, where the sun and moon represent Jacob and Leah and the stars represent their sons, fathers of the 12 tribes. The dragon's purpose was always to keep her from giving birth to the Son who will rule the nations with a rod of iron (Ps. 2), Jesus Christ our Savior.

Although he failed in that mission, he continues to pursue the woman (Israel) and her children (believers in Jesus) simply out of rage and hatred because of their part in leading rebels to repent of their rebellion and become a part of God's Kingdom once again through Jesus Christ. He knows that he can no longer stop the Savior, which he tried to do both by threatening Jesus' life (Matt. 2; Luke 4:28-30) and by trying to keep Him from fulfilling His purpose by leading Him into sin (Matt. 4:1-11). But his rage at the Savior's success and at his own pending removal from Heaven and ultimate defeat keep him lashing out at all of God's children in any way possible.

Have you ever wondered why the whole world seems to be allied against Israel? Why the UN regularly sides with nations who support and promote terrorism in condemning Israel? Why Christian churches and institutions are under increasing attack simply for existing? These things are all to be expected (Matt. 10:24-33), and we are promised that persecution will increase as the end draws near (Matt. 24:9-13).

Read Daniel 10; Eph. 6:10-24; 1 Cor. 10:20; Deut. 32:17

This brings us to a very important point as we watch what is going on in the world around us. While we may become frustrated and even angered by things that happen in the political realm, we must understand that there is more to these situations than just what we see with our eyes. There is a battle going on around us, invisible but incredibly real, that affects everything that happens here on earth.

An angel (presumably Gabriel—Daniel 8:16, 9:21) gave Daniel a glimpse into that invisible world when he came to share information with Daniel in answer to his prayer. Gabriel, God's go-to angelic messenger, tells Daniel that he was delayed for three weeks by **the prince of the kingdom of Persia** (Daniel 10:13 NASB). This is clearly not the human prince, but an angelic prince (or more precisely, a demonic one) who is one of the powers behind the Persian throne. The angel told Daniel that the archangel Michael, who is identified as having a special relationship with Israel (Dan. 10:21, 12:1) similar to the demons' relationships with the rebel kingdoms, had to come to his aid. After delivering his message, he tells Daniel that he must return to the battle with the prince of Persia and with the prince of Greece who is about to come.

Ephesians 6:12 warns us that as believers we are not ultimately battling human beings, but demonic rulers and powers who are behind human thrones all over the world. So while, as John was given the book of Revelation, Emperor Domitian might have thought that he ruled the world, he was merely a puppet whose strings were being pulled by far more cunning and powerful beings that he could not see. When we wonder why such crazy policies are being adopted by governments all over the world and why the innocent are being betrayed and believers persecuted, we must understand that our enemy is directing much of this, and his plan is not to accomplish good for humankind!

This demonic influence over the political world also stretches into the domain of false religions. In fact, the false gods, who are really demons in disguise (1 Cor. 10:20; Deut. 32:17), often prop up the rebel kings, creating a bond of loyalty with his or her subjects through a religious mythology. Demons hate human beings and are happy to torment and destroy even their own worshipers. This should help to explain the hatred and violence that flows from so many religions of the world.

One of the most heinous requirements of many of the false gods of antiquity was for human sacrifice, particularly of children (Lev. 18:21; 2 Kings 23:10). Babies were burned alive in the worship of Molech in the Valley of Hinnom, which later became the perpetually burning garbage dump called Gehenna in Jesus' day. It is no wonder that He used this terrible place to illustrate the character of Hell. Perhaps one of the most perplexing political realities for believers is the push to protect and even celebrate brutal procedures used to destroy unborn babies. When we realize who is pulling the strings for many political leaders—leaders who are full of pride and hungry for personal power—we at least have an explanation, although it offers little comfort for the horrible destruction of precious young lives.

In many ways, the last seven years of our history will find the battles now going on in invisible arenas come visibly to earth at last. Satan will no longer be satisfied with deceiving people behind the scenes. Instead, he will, through anti-Christ, openly demand to be worshiped. Angels and demons will take visible forms and be seen doing their work—the holy and the unholy—in broad daylight. For now, it is vital for believers to understand the real powers behind so many thrones and leaders and false faiths. If we fail to understand the true nature of our foe, then we will try to fight with human weapons which have no chance of success at all. Instead, we must trust and obey God and battle in prayer, in witness, and in proclamation of God's Word—spiritual weapons for a spiritual war that is invisible but oh-so-real (2 Cor. 10:4).

QUESTION 24

Who is the dragon?

Read Rev. 12:1-6

We have already covered most of the mysteries of the first part of Chapter 12. We have established, based on Joseph's dream in Gen. 37, that this woman is Israel. Her child is Jesus Christ—the One prophesied to rule the nations with a rod of iron (Psalm 2) and the One who ascended into Heaven (Acts 1). The dragon attempted to stop His mission of salvation both before He was born (by trying to get human beings to destroy themselves or to destroy Israel) and after He was born (through murder attempts by Herod, the Jews and their leaders, and by tempting Him to sin, which would have disqualified Him as our Savior). And as is plainly stated in Rev. 12:9, the dragon is none other than Satan himself, the original rebel and leader of 1/3 of Heaven's angels who joined him in his attempted coup.

Why is he represented by a dragon? The dragon is an ancient symbol of evil, and is no doubt based on some of the more massive and frightening dinosaurs that God created. Job speaks of two mighty creatures that seem certainly to have been dinosaurs, Behemoth who ruled the land (Job 40) and Leviathan who terrorized the seas (Job 41). Leviathan is even said to have breathed fire like the dragons of legend (Job 41:18-21). He is red because of the violence and bloodshed that he has inspired down through the ages (John 8:44; Rev. 17:1-6).

We will look at the symbolism of his multiple heads in an upcoming study, but the crowns he wears are in pale imitation of the Lord Jesus, who wears many crowns as King of kings and Lord of lords (Rev. 19:12). In fact, as determined as he is to usurp the Father's throne, everything that he does is in imitation and mockery of the God of the universe. In this chapter and the next we even see an unholy trinity, with Satan as the dragon in the place of God, the sea beast (anti-Christ) in the place of the Son, and the earth beast (false prophet) poorly imitating the Holy Spirit.

Satan's pursuit of God's people is part and parcel to his overall plan—to bring as many people, beloved by their Creator, down to Hell with him as possible. His attacks on Israel and the church, his attempts to thwart the mission of the Savior, and his accusations against believers all serve to bring as much condemnation as possible before his time is finished. We will look at his role as accuser after our next study.

QUESTION 25

Has the battle in Heaven al-
ready taken place?

Read Rev. 12:7-17; Luke 10:18; Job 1:6-12; Zechariah 3:1-7

This is one of the most difficult questions to answer in Revelation. Jesus told His disciples that He had personally witnessed Satan falling from Heaven to earth **like lightning** (Luke 10:18 NASB). We know that he has already rebelled against God along with 1/3 of Heaven's angels (called **stars** in Rev. 12:4). We also know, however, that he has not been permanently banned from Heaven, as he was there to accuse Job and Joshua the high priest— and, according to this passage, all believers, including each of us today.

There are two possible ways to understand the war described here. It could be a flashback of sorts to Satan's original rebellion. If so, then that would mean that, while Satan and the demons can no longer live there, Satan at least still has permission to visit from time to time.

But I think that there are several clues in this passage that indicate that this particular battle has not taken place yet. Despite what happened when Satan first rebelled, I believe that he and his demonic forces will try once more to take Heaven for themselves.

First, vs. 8 says: **...and there was no longer a place found for them in heaven** (NASB). This seems to be a permanent ban, whereas Satan currently visits Heaven to do his accusing. Second, we hear Heaven proclaim in vs. 10 that Satan's expulsion from Heaven is connected with the coming of God's Kingdom. We have already seen that God's Kingdom is not proclaimed as having come until the seventh trumpet sounds. Third, the last part of Chapter 12 indicates that after he is cast out Satan will attack Jews and Christians in a new and more terrible way since he knows that he is almost out of time. This would seem to indicate that this expulsion from Heaven is the heavenly event that contributes to the beginning of the Great Tribulation. We will see the earthly event that ultimately triggers it in Chapter 13.

All of these things taken together point to a yet future battle in Heaven where Michael and God's angels will fully defeat Satan's forces, leading God to ban him forever from even visiting Heaven to accuse believers. In retaliation, the dragon will do everything that he can on earth to hurt God's people, since he can no longer threaten them with accusations. Let's look at Satan's work as the accuser so that we will understand even better the depths of his evil and hateful nature.

FLASHBACK 8

The Accuser of the Brethren

Read Rev. 12:10-11; Job 1:6-12; Job 2:1-7;
Zechariah 3:1-7

Zechariah 3 provides one of the clearest pictures of Satan's true nature in all of Scripture. Satan is standing before God pointing to Israel's high priest Joshua and demanding that God judge both him and the nation he represents for their sins. The irony, of course, is not lost on anyone. It is Satan himself who has tempted the nation into sin. And now he is demanding that God keep His Word and judge them in keeping with His holy nature.

The Bible tells us that Satan appears **as an angel of light** (2 Cor. 11:14 NASB). He certainly presented himself to Adam and Eve as their helper trying to free them from bondage to God's "unjust" commands. But we must know that this is never his true motivation. He hates human beings precisely because God loves us so much, and his plan is always to lead us into sin and then to go immediately to the Father and demand that He hold us accountable for what we have done.

Satan knows that God is just and that He must judge sin in order to remain just. This is why Jesus had to die in order for us to be saved. The payment for sin had to be made, and only Jesus could make that payment for us. This is why God is said to be both **just and the justifier of the one who has faith in Jesus** (Rom. 3:26 NASB).

The name "Satan" itself means "adversary." The picture is of a prosecuting attorney making a formal accusation against the accused in a court of law. So accusing is very much a part of his nature. It is what he does.

So how do we respond to Satan's accusations? Well, the best news is that we have a defense attorney willing to take that task upon Himself. 1 John 2:1-2 tells us that Jesus Himself is our defense attorney (**Advocate**) as well as the One who has taken our punishment and satisfied God's righteous wrath (**propitiation**). Just as God Himself pronounced Joshua (and by extension Israel) forgiven by giving him a clean robe, so Jesus has pronounced us innocent by taking our sins upon Himself at the cross—and giving us His righteousness (and also a clean robe—Rev. 7:14) in exchange! In other words, we do not have to respond for ourselves. Jesus has spoken for us!

But there is a response required of us—not to Satan, but to Christ. This is the response of faith. This is vital to our receiving the forgiveness that He offers, but it is also incredibly important to our daily Christian walk. You see Satan knows that, whether his accusations are true (as in the case of Joshua) or false (as in the case of Job), he can keep us from serving God effectively if he can keep us trapped with his accusations instead of experiencing the freedom that we are offered in Christ (John 8:32).

Are you ever burdened with guilt as a believer? This can be either a sign of conviction by the Holy Spirit or of accusation by the enemy. Either way, we respond in faith. If it is conviction, then we will be aware of something specific that is wrong in our lives, and once we are aware of it, we will in faith repent and receive God's ready forgiveness. And we will move on in victory over that sin with His help.

If our guilt comes from the enemy, it will probably not be very specific, or else it will bring to mind some sin in our past that we have already taken to God in faith. If that is the case, and after sincere prayer God does not make us aware of any sin that requires repentance, then we will by faith receive the promise of God's Word that our past sins are forgiven and forgotten and that we can serve Him with a clear conscience because of what He has done for us in Christ. As Rev. 12:11 promises, we have overcome

our enemy and accuser because of Jesus' blood shed for us and because of our testimony of having had that blood applied to our
lives! Believing in Jesus conquers all accusations, both true and
false.

QUESTION 26

Who is this beast from the sea?

Read Rev. 13:1-3; Daniel 7:1-7

Beginning in Chapter 11, we have been looking at several important figures who will be prominent during Daniel's 70th Week. (We have speculated that perhaps these extra details about the angels and people involved in the end times were the contents of the smaller book that John was commanded to eat.) In Chapter 12, we looked at the dragon, representing Satan, the first person of the unholy trinity. In this chapter, we encounter the other two members of that evil end-times trio. These two are both human beings.

First, we meet a beast coming from the sea. The sea in Scripture represents chaos and judgment, illustrating the mess that is the Gentile nations in rebellion against God. (Although far from perfect, the Jews were nearly always more stable and moral than the Gentile nations surrounding them. They were also held to a higher degree of accountability because of their knowledge of and relationship with God.) We know that the oceans are literally the remnants of God's most terrible judgment against sinful man so far—the flood of Noah's day. This beast will be a Gentile, in many ways the ultimate Gentile. We know from Daniel 9 that he will, in one way or another, come out of the old Roman Empire.

Next, we see that he is in intimate league with the dragon. The dragon calls him from the sea and gives him his kingdom and power. He has the same heads, horns, and crowns as the dragon, indicating that he is in a sense the dragon in human flesh, again in imitation of Jesus Christ the God-man.

His body, however, is different from the dragon's. Whereas the dragon is a unified creature, the sea beast has a mish-mash of a body made up of parts of other beasts. We learn what these beasts represent in Daniel 7. There we encounter four kingdoms, the first three of which are represented by different animals. (It is significant that each of these beasts also rises out of the sea, indicating that they also are Gentile empires. All of them, including the final one led by anti-Christ, come from a place of rebellion against the rightful King of the universe.)

The first is a winged lion, which represents Babylon. (Statues of winged lions were prominent in Babylon.) The second is a bear, which represents Media-Persia, the empire which conquered Babylon during Daniel's lifetime. The third is a winged leopard, representing Greece, which in turn conquered Media-Persia. The fourth kingdom, much like this sea-beast, is a combination of the others and represents the Roman Empire in both its past and future incarnations.

This sea-beast has the body of the leopard, the feet of the bear, and the mouth of the lion. It is thus a combination of the previous world empires joined together, united under one terrible but charismatic leader. This sea-beast thus represents the person that we often call anti-Christ, the final world leader who will bring all of the world together against the rightful King (2 Thess. 2:3-4; 1 John 2:18). We will look more closely at what his heads and crowns represent in Chapter 17.

FLASHBACK 9

Daniel's Visions

Read Daniel 2

It is almost impossible to understand the progression of world empires leading up to the final empire under anti-Christ without reading the book of Daniel. God revealed the succession of world-dominating empires to King Nebuchadnezzar of Babylon through Daniel as He gave the prophet understanding of the king's dream.

In his dream, Nebuchadnezzar saw a huge statue made of various metals, starting at the top with gold and ending at the feet which were iron mixed with clay. God revealed to the king that he was seeing the future—a succession of world-dominating empires, beginning with his own. These kingdoms would decrease in culture and grandeur even as they increased in brute strength. (Gold is the most valuable but also the softest of these metals; iron is the least valuable but also the strongest.) We know from history that Babylon was overtaken and absorbed by Media-Persia, which was in turn overtaken and absorbed by Greece. Rome came along later, incorporating all of these previous empires into its own, and then later was divided into two kingdoms before (temporarily) losing its prominence on the world stage.

But God also revealed something else to Nebuchadnezzar that is very important. During the time of these four kingdoms, God promised to do all that is necessary to establish His everlasting Kingdom. This act is represented by the **stone...cut out without hands** (Daniel 2:34 NASB) crushing the other kingdoms until no trace of them remains. This stone represents Jesus, who would come during the time of the Roman Empire and accomplish salvation and offer it to all people—an opportunity to repent of our rebellion and once again become citizens of the true and everlasting Kingdom. Daniel makes clear to Nebuchadnezzar that, once this Kingdom comes in its fullness, it will never be threatened or rivalled again!

Read Daniel 7

In Daniel 7, Daniel once again sees the four successive kingdoms, this time represented by beasts. The winged lion, representing Babylon, lost its wings and was raised up on two legs like a man, probably referring to Nebuchadnezzar's humbling and eventual belief in the true and living God as described in Daniel 4. The lopsided bear represented Media-Persia, always an unbalanced kingdom dominated by the Persian side. The three ribs in its mouth may have represented Egypt, Assyria, and Babylon, the three world empires that came before it. The winged leopard represented Greece, who under Alexander conquered the world with almost blinding speed. Alexander only lived into his early thirties, but had conquered most of the known world by that time. The four heads represent the four generals who eventually got control of different parts of Alexander's empire after his death.

The fourth beast is not really compared to a known creature, but is described in powerful and dreadful terms. It is also revealed that eventually ten kingdoms (represented by ten horns) will come out of this empire, and that in the end they will be united in service to anti-Christ, represented by the **little horn**. Rev. 17:12-13 tells us that these kings have not yet arisen, but will come out of what once was the Roman Empire, which dominated the world in John's day. The reign of anti-Christ, whose mouth will be full of blasphemies, will be brought to an end by the **Ancient of Days** Himself through the person of His Son, Jesus Christ, the **Son of man**, whose Kingdom will never end.

Read Daniel 8

The vision given to Daniel in Chapter 8 focuses on just two of these kingdoms—Media-Persia and Greece. These were the two soon-coming Kingdoms, as Babylon was in her last years under Belshazzar. Daniel would also serve the Medes and Persians, and some of the visions in the book of Daniel were given to him during that time.

He first sees a ram with two unbalanced horns, once again representing the unbalanced kingdom of Media-Persia. A kingdom represented by a flying goat brings the ram's kingdom to an end, but is soon itself broken up into four smaller, weaker kingdoms which were eventually absorbed into Rome.

Out of one of the four lesser kingdoms would come another horn, a ruler who would have a great and terrible impact upon Israel (**the Beautiful Land**). This was a prophecy of Antiochus Epiphanes, the latter name meaning "god manifest." This wicked and arrogant king took this name for himself, and eventually desecrated the Jewish temple, offering a pig on the altar and demanding that the Jews worship the Greek gods instead of the true and living God. Under the Maccabees, the Jews were eventually able to gain their independence from Antiochus and his kingdom, if only for a short time before being absorbed into the Roman Empire. But for 2300 days, Antiochus severely persecuted Israel, murdering thousands and dividing the nation into Hellenists who were willing to adopt at least some parts of Greek culture and the loyal Jews who refused to compromise. We still see divisions between these two groups in the early church in Acts 6.

Antiochus is important because he was a prophetic picture of the future anti-Christ. His desecration of the temple was the first **abomination of desolation**. His slaughter of Jews who refused to worship him and the Greek gods foreshadows the same blasphemous requirements that will be made by anti-Christ during the Great Tribulation. Daniel 11 gives an incredibly detailed prophecy of Antiochus' campaigns against Israel and Egypt, with the focus eventually changing in the latter verses of that chapter to the future anti-Christ. These two men are spiritual twins separated by centuries of time. Much like John the Baptist and the future witness who both come in the spirit and power of Elijah, the future anti-Christ will have much in common with this monster from Israel's past.

The prophecies that God gave Daniel give us a detailed description of the empires of history that will lead up to and play a part in the final world empire under anti-Christ. This last empire will be the fulfillment of all that these other empires could not quite accomplish—total world domination--under Satan's most trusted servant. While many have demanded worship and obedience, anti-Christ will receive the worship of the vast majority of the world's citizens. The inflated egos that plague all of the world's most powerful leaders will find their ultimate fulfillment in the final world leader. The true arrogance of all of us rebellious creatures will finally be revealed in all of its ugliness and violence during the Great Tribulation.

QUESTION 27

*What event on earth sets off the
sea beast's reign of terror?*

Read Revelation 13:3-10; Daniel 9:27; Rev. 17:7-13

Daniel 9:27 tells us that the sea-beast/anti-Christ will have two distinct personalities during two periods of his seven-year reign. While he will always be a warrior (as opposed to the more "spiritual" earth beast), he will begin his reign by including negotiation and statesmanship in his repertoire. His relationship with the Jews will begin in an apparently positive manner. He will negotiate a covenant agreement with the majority in Israel at the beginning of Daniel's 70th Week, one which will apparently benefit Israel greatly, perhaps even giving her a brief period of what looks like peace despite the enemies that surround her.

But in the middle of that seven-year period—very suddenly according to Jesus (Matt. 24:15-19)—he will betray the Jews and set himself up to be worshiped in their temple, much as Antiochus Epiphanes did more than 2,000 years ago. He will openly claim to be god and will make terrible claims about the true and living God. (Rev. 13 and the "little horn" references in Daniel emphasize that he has a horribly arrogant and blasphemous tongue. It is impossible to be any more arrogant than to claim to deserve the throne of the rightful King!) Satan's practice of deception and staying under the radar will all go out the window, as his chief officer on earth directs the world to worship himself and the dragon.

We have already seen that the event in Heaven that leads to this dramatic increase in anger and violence on the part of the dragon is when he and his armies are defeated and finally banned from God's presence forever. But there is also an event that happens on earth at about the same time which changes the tone of anti-Christ from subtle politician to arrogant and blasphemous dictator. Anti-Christ is murdered!

Revelation 13:3 says that one of his heads receives a fatal wound which is then healed. Rev. 17:10 says that the seven heads of the beast represent 7 rulers or kings, 5 of whom had already died by John's time, one of whom ruled in John's day, and one of whom was yet to come. This seventh is the future anti-Christ, and this is the head that receives the deadly wound. We know that he is the wounded head because the world is so impressed by his resurrection that they worship him and the dragon. This is yet another act meant to imitate the living God who raised His Son from the dead, and it is likely that many in this future time will see the sea-beast as the "real Messiah" because this happens.

After his resurrection, he will become angry and more openly arrogant, demanding to be worshiped and persecuting Israel and the church with renewed passion and energy, making them enemies of the empire. Perhaps he will blame a Jew or a Christian for the attempted assassination in order to further justify his rampage. But I believe that there is something more than just an angry man behind his new violent and hateful demeanor. I believe that a new being comes into the picture during this time who will ramp up the evil in a spectacular way.

Rev. 17:9-11 says this:

"Here is the mind which has wisdom. The seven heads are seven mountains on which the woman sits, and they are seven kings; five have fallen, one is, the other has not yet come; and when he comes, he must remain a little while. "The beast which was and is not, is himself also an eighth and is one of the seven, and he goes to destruction...." (NASB)

Vs. 11 may be the most confounding verse in the entire Bible, but I think when we properly understand it, it will help several things in Revelation to come into focus. This passage tells us that the seven heads represent two things. We will talk about the first when we study Babylon in Chapter 17. But the second thing the heads represent, as we have already mentioned, are seven historic rulers of seven world empires. We know from Daniel that the last five are the kings of: Babylon, Media-Persia, Greece, Rome, and the second Roman Empire of anti-Christ. Because all of these were empires that dominated Israel, it is probably safe to assume that the first two are Egypt and Assyria. Other nations, such as the Philistines and Syrians, fought fiercely against Israel, but no others were world empires.

Again, John was told that five of those rulers were already gone before 100 AD. One of them, the emperor of Rome, was alive and known well by John. But one was yet to come, and would rule only **a little while**—most likely referring to his reign of terror during the 3 ½ years of the Great Tribulation. He then gives us several details of that ruler that we must fit together:

He is a **beast**—clearly the sea-beast

He **was and is not**—he had been on earth at some
      point before John's day, but was not on earth at
      that time

He is one of those seven kings represented by the
      heads

He is also an eighth—a separate ruler altogether

So how can all of these things be?

There is only one solution that I believe checks all of these boxes. Because he is called a beast, the ruler described here must be the yet future anti-Christ, the sea-beast of Revelation 13 and the seventh head. That makes him the seventh of those seven kings, just as John is told. The other two points are the curious ones. He had lived on earth at some point in the past. He was not living on earth in John's day. But he will live again in the future and will be at the same time both the seventh of these rulers (the seventh head) AND a totally separate ruler—the eighth. How is that possible?

Do you remember our dilemma in Chapter 11? The two witness will be killed by the **beast that comes up out of the abyss** (Rev. 11:7 NASB). We noted there that that description does not fit any one being. There is an angel of the abyss, a terrible demon captain that has been imprisoned for centuries (Rev. 9:11); but he is never called a beast. And there are the sea and earth beasts from Chapter 13, neither of whom come out of the abyss. Both of the beasts are human beings, while those imprisoned in the abyss are fallen angels who once freely roamed the earth. That description then must mean that this eighth ruler, who is also one of the seven, is a combination of the sea-beast (the human anti-Christ) and the Destroyer who is released from the abyss, apparently a little ahead of the locust-like demons who are released later after the rapture of believers.

When do these two come together? I believe that once anti-Christ is killed, his body is either revived or reanimated by this terrible demon from the pit, who then lives up to his name in both Hebrew and Greek, striking out against and attempting to destroy everything good that God has created! This is the only way that I can imagine that he could be both the seventh—anti-Christ—and an eighth ruler, and that he could have been on earth in the past and at the same time be a human being who is yet to be born (at least in John's day). It would also explain his extreme rage. After all, God had imprisoned him and the other demons because they had tried to move past the boundaries that He had set for their evil, trying to destroy humanity before God could bring us a Savior. He has already shown that he is full of hatred and violence; his work through anti-Christ will be in that same spirit.

This would also explain one other thing. As far as I know, Satan does not have the power to give life. I do not believe that he can actually resurrect anti-Christ as God did His only begotten Son. Unless he is able to somehow revive the human anti-Christ soon after death, this would leave the sea beast as a sort of zombie, a dead human body possessed and reanimated by one of the most evil of all of the rebel angels. If he is somehow revived and still alive inside his body, the Destroyer will possess and control him, although not in a way that is really that much different from his own character and heart.

There is one other important detail that I want us to file away at this point. When the reanimated anti-Christ demands the world's worship, he gets it for the most part. True Christians and faithful Jews will not comply, and he will punish them at every opportunity. But he will be worshipped by everyone whose name has not been written in the Book of Life from the very beginning. While I do believe that God allows us to choose to receive or to reject His gift of salvation, I also believe that He has always known what choice we will make. Scripture tells us that His foreknowledge precedes predestination (Rom. 8:29).

This is very important as we look forward to the Millennial Kingdom which follows Christ's victory at Armageddon. We know that believers will be raptured into their eternal bodies when Christ returns during the Great Tribulation (Matt. 24:29-31; 1 Thess. 4:13-18). Jewish believers will be protected and will populate Messiah's promised Kingdom as mortals during the Millennium (Rev. 12:6; 14:1-5). Everyone who takes the beast's mark will be destroyed by the bowl judgments or at Armageddon (Rev. 19:20-21). Yet the Old Testament Millennial prophecies frequently mention people of other nations coming to Jerusalem during that time period (Is. 2:3). This must mean that a number of people from many nations who had not yet trusted Christ before the rapture, and yet who also had not taken the mark of the beast, will escape anti-Christ's wrath, and will enter the Millennial Kingdom as citizens of many Gentile nations (Daniel 7:11-12). So, while they had not yet trusted Christ before the rapture, those who will believe in Christ after the rapture are still recorded in the Book of Life because God knew the decision that they would eventually make. This detail is not directly described in God's Word, but other details—particularly the presence of mortal Gentiles during the Millennium—make something like this necessary.

QUESTION 28

Who is the earth-beast?

Read Rev. 13:11-17

John saw **another beast**, but unlike the sea-beast (or any of Daniel's beasts), this one originates on dry land. At the very least we know that this beast is not part of the succession of world leaders and empires that make up the sea-beast. In fact, this beast turns out not to be a political leader at all. He is the high priest of anti-Christ's final false religion. He resembles a lamb with two horns, indicating that he, too, is trying to look like Jesus. But his five fewer horns betray the fact that he is no match for the Son of God in power or authority. Also unlike Jesus, who spoke only the words that the Father gave Him (John 8:28; John 12:50), this beast speaks with the voice of the dragon.

He performs signs that prove that he has supernatural power. He uses those signs, as well as the power of his dragon voice, to deceive people into worshiping the sea-beast as their god. Scripture is not completely clear about what powers Satan and his demons actually have, or what abilities they can lend to human beings. In the case of Egypt's practitioners of the black arts, they could mimic the first few signs that God gave Moses to perform, but were quickly overwhelmed and overpowered—not by the power of Moses, but by the power of God working through him. So we know that demons can perform at least a limited number of supernatural signs, but that their power is no match for God's power. Satan is not God's evil opposite; Michael is the proper match for him. There is no opposite for God, because God our Creator (and theirs) is unique in power and in wisdom. There is none like Him! (Exodus 8:10; 1 Samuel 2:2)

It is unclear whether or not there is any other significance to the fact that this second beast comes from the earth. Since the sea-beast rises from the sea, whose chaos represents the Gentile nations, then it could be possible that the earth-beast is an unbelieving Jew. If he is from the same ethnic group as our Savior, then this might also explain his lamb-like appearance. But we are not told specifically that this is true in Scripture, so we must leave this to speculation—until the events actually happen.

The earth-beast basically functions as the unholy spirit in this unholy trinity. Just as the Holy Spirit exalts and testifies about Christ (John 15:26), so this beast exalts and leads others to worship anti-Christ. The sea-beast is limited to being in one place at a time, but the earth-beast is able to create lifelike images of the sea-beast that can be distributed across the world and are even able to punish those who refuse to worship him. This is in mockery of the Holy Spirit's ability to be everywhere at once, something that Jesus told His disciples would be to their advantage after He went back to Heaven (John 16:7). And if the sea-beast really is only reanimated and not fully revived, the images created by the earth-beast take on an even more important role, as the decaying body of the sea-beast will eventually need to be kept from public view. The Holy Spirit is also the power behind miracles performed by believers through spiritual gifts, something else that the earth-beast seems to be trying to imitate here.

Possibly the most intriguing duty of the earth-beast will be his charge to mark all of those loyal to the beast with a number that represents his name. This mark, probably the most well-known prophecy in the book of Revelation, will be placed on the forehead or hand and will be necessary to do any kind of business, including buying food to eat. Many have speculated about how the mark will be delivered—tattoo, laser, implanted chip—and what it will actually look like. But all that the Bible tells us is that it will contain either the beast's name or a number that is synonymous with his name.

Many languages assign numerical values to different letters. We are probably most familiar with the Roman version of this, ironically enough, where V = 5, X = 10, etc. It seems likely that it is the numerical value of the letters in his name which will add up to 666. Beyond this, anything that we say about this mark can only be speculation. And this is exactly what we should expect, since we will not know the name until the time has arrived.

QUESTION 29

What is the Lamb doing with the 144,000 on Mt. Zion?

Read Rev. 14:1-5; Zechariah 13:8-9; Zech. 14:1-8

We have not seen the 144,000 for some time. Most likely they have been among the Israelites protected in the wilderness (Rev. 12:6) from Satan's wrath and God's judgments. Here they are called **first fruits**, which describes the very earliest fruit born by a crop before the main harvest arrives. They are thus not the entire saved group of Israel (Rom. 11:26), but the first to be saved. They will certainly have a strong influence on the rest.

Zechariah 13-14 tells us that armies will gather against Israel just before God comes to establish His eternal Kingdom. Two thirds of the Jews remaining in Israel will be killed, but one third will become the remnant of those whom God rescues. It is unclear whether this entire third has already been taken to the wilderness for protection or whether this surviving remnant will join those who fled there. Either way, the survivors will be the group that fulfills the prophecy of Rom. 11:26 promising that all Israel—all that remains of Israel on earth—will come to salvation in Jesus. It seems certain that these 12 groups of 12,000 from each tribe will take the lead in bringing that group to faith in Christ and in discipling them at the very beginning of the Millennial Kingdom. (This discipleship will not continue during most of that time according to Jer. 31:34, as everyone in Israel will know God personally and well!)

Just as the beast has marked his followers, these men will be marked by God as belonging to Him. They will bear His name, just as the followers of the beast wear his. Unlike the beast's followers, they will be pure—either virgins or men who have not engaged in sex outside of marriage. (Remember that immorality is a big part of the worship of false gods who are actually demons in disguise.) They will also be completely truthful in their speech. But lest we think that these men have achieved this on their own, note carefully the repeated reminder that they have been **purchased from the earth**. These men will be repentant and saved sinners, dependent totally on God's grace just as we are today.

They are also privileged with the ability to learn a new song that comes from Heaven. Only they can sing it. This is a picture of the intimacy they have with God—both Father and Son—and of the special place in history that they occupy. All of the first believers were Jews, but this quickly changed as Gentiles joined the church and the majority of Jews rejected the message of salvation through Christ. Jewish believers since that time have waited for the day when their people will come en masse to Jesus (Rom. 9:1-5). These 144,000 men will get that wonderful time in history started.

It is also significant that they are with Jesus on Mt. Zion. In John's day, that name was used to describe the temple mount. Anti-Christ has dominated and desecrated that area for almost 3 ½ years by this point (and Gentiles have done so now for centuries since the 70 AD), but this group is defiantly standing there announcing that that sacred place is about to be returned to its original owner for good! While all of the world's armies will soon be piling in to defend anti-Christ's hold on the city, they cannot stop this (by comparison) relatively small army of believers following the King of kings. There is no indication that any battle takes place at this point—although their song must sound like nails on a chalkboard to the beast and his followers--but instead there seems simply to be the declaration that the King has returned with some of His most faithful followers to claim what belongs to Him!

QUESTION 30

What is the purpose of these three angels?

Read Rev. 14:6-13

Isn't God's patience amazing? It would seem by now that He has sufficiently demonstrated His power and sovereignty over the earth. He has made the choice given to all human beings very clear. But before the final bowl judgments are poured out, He makes one more set of announcements meant to warn unbelievers and to comfort any on earth who have come to Christ since the rapture.

First, a high-flying angel once again preaches the Gospel message to everyone left on earth. Since God's Word never returns to Him without accomplishing His purpose (Is. 55:10-11), it seems certain that some will be brought to salvation through this angel's ministry.

Next, a different angel declares that Babylon, the capitol of anti-Christ's empire, has fallen. We will look more closely at Babylon in Chapter 17, but this announcement warns those who are enamored with this rebellious world system that their end will not be a desirable one. A third angel then describes exactly what that end will be: unending, burning torment right beside the beast and false prophet who have promised them freedom and happiness in exchange for their worship.

Then a quick word of encouragement is added for the persecuted church. Those who die for their faith in Christ will be blessed with both rest and reward. It may seem like a frightening decision to make with a gun pointed at your head, but God promises that it will be by far the best choice for us for eternity.

God is so faithful throughout His Word to remind us again and again what our choice is—His eternal Kingdom or Satan's temporary rebel outfit—and what the rewards of those two choices are. Even at the end, God is making sure that both the choice and the consequences are clear. We must never take for granted how much time we have left to decide.

QUESTION 31

*What event is being fore-
shadowed here?*

Read Rev. 14:14-20; Daniel 7:13-14

As soon as the warning is given, John then sees a preview of the harvest. He sees **one like a son of man** sitting on a cloud, a crown on His head and an instrument for harvesting grain in His hand. This is clearly a reference to Daniel's vision in Daniel 7, where **one like a son of Man** comes on a cloud before the Ancient of Days and is worshiped and given an everlasting kingdom. Since the passage from Daniel is a prophesy about Jesus, this reference tells us that this crowned Person is Jesus Christ as well.

Some Bible students have objected to seeing this person as the Christ since an angel seems to give Him an order in vs. 15. But rather than seeing this as a command, we can understand it as the angel communicating a message from God the Father. The fact that the angel comes out of the temple in Heaven tells us that he has come from the Father's presence. Jesus said that only the Father knew the exact day and time of His return (Matt. 24:36), so this information had to be shared with Christ at some point in time.

There seem to be two reapings. The first is conducted by Jesus; the second by an angel. The first likely looks back to the rapture, where believers were taken up. As we saw, the removal of the church and protection of the remnant of Israel was necessary before God poured out His judgment, which is clearly the point of the second reaping. The fact that the Lord is pictured doing the reaping reminds us that what we do with Him determines where we will spend eternity and which harvest will include us.

The second no doubt refers to the judgment of the lost, especially the final decisive defeat of anti-Christ and his forces that comes at the battle of Armageddon. The revelation that there will be enough blood in that valley to come up to the bridles of horses tells us that untold millions of enemy soldiers will meet their doom on that great and terrible day.

QUESTION 32

What happens in Heaven as the last judgments are brought out?

Read Rev. 15.

God has been incredibly patient in holding back His wrath, giving everyone ample opportunity to choose to become part of His Kingdom through repentance and faith. But now Heaven takes a deep breath as that patience has finally come to an end. Even the trumpet judgments were only partial judgments and were stretched out over some time, giving those feeling their fury opportunities to repent if they had not taken the beast's mark on forehead or hand. But now we see judgments in shallow bowls, bowls that can be quickly flipped over and dumped onto a defenseless earth. And this is exactly what happens.

Earth's redeemed stand on the sea of glass around God's throne. They play harps and sing the song of deliverance that Moses sang after God saved His people from slavery in Egypt. They also sing the Lamb's song, the song of salvation and deliverance from sin. These are the two most prominent songs of the Old and New Testaments, respectively. They praise the rightful King as the only one worthy of worship and praise—and they rejoice that now the whole world will be forced to admit that long-denied truth.

The angels carrying these judgments come out of Heaven's holiest place. God's wrath and judgment is not like man's; it comes not from a place of hatred or revenge, but from a place of truth and justice. It is holy, not selfish or petty. The angels are dressed like priests, and perhaps they are the priests of Heaven's temple. Even the awesome duty assigned to these angels is ultimately an act of worship to a Holy God.

Just as happened when the earthly tabernacle and temple were dedicated (Ex. 40:34-35; 2 Chron. 5:11-14), Heaven's temple fills with a thick cloud of smoke produced by God's own glory and power. It is so dense and strong that it prevents anyone from entering the temple until this final work of judgment is done. This is a time of awe, wonder, and joy in Heaven—a day anticipated for centuries, delayed only by God's mercy and grace. But now the day has come.

QUESTION 33

What happens as these bowls of judgment are poured out on the earth?

Read Rev. 16; Rev. 8:7-12

Three of the first four bowl judgments are related to three of the first four trumpet judgments. The main difference is that they are complete, where the trumpet judgments left room for life and hope. The first trumpet judgment was hail and fire that burned 1/3 of the world's plant life. The first bowl judgment is terrible sores on everyone who is part of anti-Christ's rebel kingdom.

The second and third of both the trumpet and bowl judgments affect earth's waters, the seas and the freshwater. 1/3 of life in the waters is destroyed by the trumpet judgments. All aquatic life dies as a result of the bowl judgments. In fact, when the fresh waters turn to blood, reminiscent of the plague on the Nile delivered through Moses, one of God's angels declares His justice in repaying those who had shed the blood of believers with more blood than they could imagine—and nothing but blood to drink. An "amen" comes from the altar. Could this be the martyrs under the altar (Rev. 6:9) raising their voices in agreement?

The fourth trumpet judgment saw 1/3 of heaven's lights—sun, moon, and stars—dimmed. (It is unclear whether this is temporary or whether it lasts for the duration of Daniel's 70th Week.) The fourth bowl judgment sees the sun's heat intensify, scorching and burning the beast's followers. The response of the beast's followers is typical of those who have hardened their hearts against the true and living God—blasphemies and cursing rather than repentance and faith. There is no doubt now left about God's existence or His power, but the worshipers of the beast continue to reject His Kingship over their lives. They are resigned to eternal misery with the masters that they have chosen.

The fifth bowl judgment brings debilitating darkness on the kingdom of the beast. This no doubt makes everything extremely difficult for the beast's followers. It may also bring an incredible night of cold after the intensely hot plague of the fourth bowl judgment. If you have ever experienced a serious sunburn and then spent the night under cool air conditioning, you know how this change causes you to chill and suffer even more. All of these pains together—the sores, the burns, and the darkness—cause them to continue to curse God for judging them.

This is an important thing for us to note. The redeemed understand that God's judgment is just and right. They also know that they have escaped that judgment not because they are superior to the lost, but because of God's great mercy and grace. The lost, however, feel that God's judgments are not just. After all, they are not *that* bad. (Even when they have been killing believers and partying over their dead bodies!) Hard, cynical hearts reject judgment. Tender, repentant hearts acknowledge that it had to eventually fall because God is just and holy.

The sixth bowl judgment dries up the Euphrates, clearing the path for all the eastern kings to marshal their forces to join anti-Christ in opposition to Christ and His armies. I believe that, especially with the amount of blood that will fill the valley, there will likely be hundreds of millions if not billions of soldiers who come to join anti-Christ in this final battle. On the surface, this act might actually seem like doing these armies a favor. But as we shall soon see, they are being led to a final and terrible end. It reminds us of Christ's words that the path to destruction is by far the wider and easier path (Matt. 7:13-14)—until that end is reached.

Not only is the path cleared, but invitations are issued. Demons are sent to impress nations that might be otherwise reluctant with impressive supernatural feats. Perhaps this gives these nations greater confidence that the beast has more power at his disposal than he really does. They have already been given more than a taste of God's power. It may take some convincing to persuade some of them to march to Jerusalem. They are all led to the Valley of Megiddo surrounding Jerusalem—the valley that will soon run five feet deep with their own blood.

The final bowl judgment sets the stage for the final battle. The Father declares that, with the pouring out of this bowl, His judgments against the rebel kingdoms are done. A deadly storm begins, accompanied by the worst earthquake in all of human history. This earthquake will divide Jerusalem into three parts, and will actually help some of the Jews to escape the battle (Zech. 14:4-5). The world will change dramatically, as islands and mountains disappear, along with all of the world's cities other than Jerusalem. This includes the great city of anti-Christ, here called Babylon. We will learn more about its identity in the next chapter. Perhaps the most astounding part of the storm are the hundred-pound hailstones that will fall, doing unimaginable damage to people, animals, and buildings. I have seen golf ball sized hail and the damage that can result from that. I have heard of softball sized hail, and can only imagine how devastating that must be. Hundred-pound hailstones are beyond my imagination; people living under the beast at the very end will not have to use their imaginations!

QUESTION 34

Who is the harlot riding the beast?

Read Rev. 17; 1 Peter 5:13; Zechariah 5:5-11; Gen. 11:1-6

John was shown a vision of a prostitute riding a scarlet beast. We know from verses 7-11 that the beast is the sea-beast/anti-Christ. The woman is dressed in the finest clothing and jewelry, and carries a golden cup filled with abominations—things God hates—and the results of her gross immorality. Bible students debate whether her prostitution and immorality are to be taken literally or whether they represent spiritual prostitution, the worship of false gods eventually culminating in the beast. There is really no need to choose one or the other, since the demons behind the idols worshiped all over the world have demanded illicit sexual acts through both male and female prostitutes as part of their worship. In other words, spiritual adultery results in physical adultery and fornication. Her immorality, spiritual and physical, has corrupted all the nations of the world.

This harlot is said to sit atop many waters, indicating that she rules over the Gentile nations (Rev. 17:15). The fact that she rides the beast, which is a combination of all of the world-dominating empires of history, shows us that she is built on all of those rebel empires throughout history. She is said to be **drunk with the blood of the saints, and with the blood of the witnesses of Jesus** (Rev. 17:6 NASB). Throughout its history, the city represented by this harlot has killed both Jews and Christians.

Her name is conveniently written on her forehead, although it is said to be a mystery: **"BABYLON THE GREAT, THE**

MOTHER OF HARLOTS AND OF THE ABOMINATIONS OF THE EARTH." (Rev. 17:5 NASB) (A mystery in Scripture is something that God has had to reveal in order for us to understand or know it. The church, for example, was a mystery during the Old Testament period. It was revealed by God through Jesus Christ.) In this case, the mystery is that this city is not literally Babylon, which was destroyed years ago. It is, however, the spiritual heir to that city, where organized idolatry and rebellion against God began (Gen. 11:1-6; Shinar is the plain upon which Babylon was eventually built). Zechariah foresaw a time when wickedness would once again be centered in spiritual Babylon.

Is there any other evidence in this passage that this harlot represents a city other than literal Babylon? How do we know that she represents a city at all? The last verse of this chapter answers both of these questions. **"The woman whom you saw is the great city, which reigns over the kings of the earth."** (Rev. 17:18 NASB) The angel tells John that the woman does indeed represent a city which (present tense) rules the entire world. In John's day, this was clearly Rome. This harlot is the city from which anti-Christ will one day rule the world—a revived Rome. (Vs. 6 tells us that the city is built on seven hills or mountains, which was true of Rome. And Peter refers to Rome as Babylon in 1 Peter 5:13.)

But Rome will not rule the world alone. She will have allied with her ten other kingdoms who share the beast's hatred for the King of kings and His followers. These 10 kingdoms will be in addition to the five world empires (represented by five of the heads) upon which the final world empire is built. This is clear since the horns are separate from the heads, but all are part of the same beast (which represents both anti-Christ and his empire). John is also told that the horns have not yet been given kingdoms, while the nations represented by the heads have already existed as kingdoms in the past. These ten are also said to exist for only a short time (**one hour** Rev. 17:12 NASB), whereas the other great empire have endured after having been absorbed into the empires following them for centuries.

Daniel saw these same kingdoms also represented by

horns (Daniel 7:7-8, 23-24). He adds two details to the account here in Revelation. First, the angel tells him that the ten kingdoms represented by the horns sprung up from the fourth beast kingdom—the first Roman Empire. Thus these ten kingdoms will all have at one time been a part of the Roman Empire, possibly placing them in modern-day Europe. Second, Daniel saw the little horn representing anti-Christ pulling three of these horns out by the roots. This tells us that, while all ten kingdoms will eventually be united in purpose under the sea-beast, three of them will come to that point by force. (It is tempting to see these three as Babylon, Media-Persia, and Greece, which were forcibly conquered and became a part of the Roman Empire. But they actually conquered one another and were not all individually conquered by Rome. This still could be true, but I lean toward the 10 kingdoms represented by the horns being ten different kingdoms altogether.)

One final detail must be mentioned. While the ten kingdoms and anti-Christ are all agreed in their hatred for and rebellion against the Lamb, they actually are not especially loyal to one another. In fact, they will be the instruments of God's judgment against the city of Rome! They will destroy it in one day. We know that from the mid-point of Daniel's 70th Week anti-Christ will set himself up in the Jerusalem temple, claiming to be god. Rome will apparently fall out of favor at this point and will eventually be destroyed by the coalition of kings working with anti-Christ. Rev. 16:19 tells us that this happens when the seventh bowl of God's wrath is poured out, just before the final battle of Armageddon.

We should not be surprised that those aligned with anti-Christ turn on their own capitol city. As we saw in Revelation 9, Satan is not concerned with the well-being even of those who worship him. Rebellion is the result of a desire to be one's own master, and it claims no loyalty outside of what serves its selfish purposes. So this spirit of rebellion opposes not only the rightful King, but also anyone or anything that is not currently helping the rebel achieve his or her goals.

QUESTION 35

*Why does God call His people
to come out of Babylon?*

Read Rev. 18:1-19:6; Romans 7:14-25

A popular song from "West Side Story" called "Tonight" has two characters singing their own perspectives on what is going on in their lives. Revelation 18 (and the first part of Chapter 19) is such a song, with Heaven rejoicing over and Earth mourning the same event—the sudden destruction of the capitol of the rebel kingdom of Babylon. Earth mourns for the place where riches were gained and immoral thrills celebrated. Heaven rejoices that the heart of the rebel kingdom, stained with the blood of God's children, has finally received her comeuppance.

As in Chapter 17, much emphasis is placed on the sudden and fiery destruction of Babylon (Rev. 17:16, 18:8). This may well mean that terrible weapons will be used by the beast and his allies to level the city. After she is destroyed, her true nature will shine through. She had dressed herself in fine clothing and expensive jewelry, but in reality she was a dark and ugly place, inhabited by demons. Once her façade is removed on the day of her destruction, her true character will be revealed.

Knowing that Babylon represents Rome—both the city and the empire—would have made this a very comforting passage for believers in John's day, since persecution and death were being poured out of Rome against believers. But this passage also tells us that Babylon is more than just one city in one period of time.

125

The code name "Babylon" also tells us this. Babylon represents the kingdom of anti-Christ, the chief rebel kingdom to which all others on earth are joined. End-times Rome will simply be the final and most complete physical manifestation of this reality on earth. Every other empire of man that has exalted itself is part of this rebel kingdom, as is every individual who chooses, just as did Adam and Eve before us, to become gods and masters of our own lives, not trusting that the true and living God has our best interest at heart.

This is why God interrupts this song of Babylon's destruction to call all believers out of that place. It is not so much a call to physically leave Rome—although this may have also been wise considering the persecution going on at this time. But more than that, it was and is a call to true believers not to allow themselves to be dragged down by the temporary pleasures and pride of the rebel kingdom. Believers are still human beings, experiencing an ongoing duel between our old and new natures (Rom. 7). Any time we are tempted back toward rebellion, we become less effective as ambassadors for Christ's Kingdom. And we lose the joy of our new life in Christ.

God is calling us, all of us, to completely abandon the rebel kingdom that is this world system. Not to leave the world before He calls us home, but to refuse to be consumed with this world's priorities and standards. Instead, we are to be singularly focused on God and on the joys and requirements of citizenship in His Kingdom. And if we find ourselves too comfortable in Babylon for too long, we need to think seriously about whether or not we have truly been born again into Christ's Kingdom at all.

QUESTION 36

What will the Battle of Arma-geddon be like?

Read Revelation 19:11-21; Zechariah 13:8-14:15

Remember what has happened up to this point. The last seven years of this age of earth's history begins with a covenant between anti-Christ and the majority in Israel (Dan. 9:27). But all around the world there is a great deal of fighting, disease, and death. As the opening of the seals progress, 1 out of every 4 people on earth ends up dead.

At the mid-point of this seven-year period, catastrophic events in Heaven and on earth cause a dramatic change in anti-Christ and in his rebel kingdom, physically centered in Rome but spiritually called Babylon. First, Satan and his angels attempt one more coup in Heaven. They are turned away and banned from Heaven forever. Full of wrath, Satan, the dragon, pours his anger out on the earth, specifically targeting Israel and the church. At the same time on earth anti-Christ is killed (almost certainly in Jerusalem) and inhabited by a terrible demon who has been set free from the pit. Whether he actually comes back to life or his body is simply animated by this demon, he takes on a new and terrible persona. He immediately takes over the temple, setting up an image of himself and demanding to be worshipped. He strikes out at those living in Jerusalem (possibly under the guise of punishing his killers) so severely and so suddenly that Jesus warned those who will be alive in that day to leave the city immediately without stopping for anything.

Anti-Christ continues to persecute and kill Jews and Christians until God finally intervenes, sealing a representative group of 144,000 Jews and protecting others in a wilderness area, possibly in modern-day Jordan (Edom, Moab, and parts of Ammon—Daniel 11:41). At some point unknown to anyone but the Father (Matt. 24:36), God interrupts the Great Tribulation (the last 3 ½ years of Daniel's 70th Week) by initiating dramatic signs in the Heavens, signaling the beginning of His wrath against the rebel kingdom. Jesus appears in the sky, and followers of anti-Christ try to hide, knowing their judgment is at hand. At this time, Jesus sends His angels to gather the persecuted church, taking all current believers to Heaven. He resurrects all the saved of history also at this time, and the resurrected and the raptured receive their eternal bodies (1 Thess. 4:13-18).

As soon as the sealed and the saved are safe from harm, God begins to pour out His judgments against anti-Christ's kingdom. These are the trumpet and bowl judgments. As the bowl judgments near their end, the unholy trinity (the dragon, anti-Christ, and the false prophet) send demons to summon all of the world's armies that are loyal to them—perhaps hundreds of millions or even billions of men—to Jerusalem for battle. Christ, meanwhile, has met with the 144,000 and probably with the rest of the remnant of Israel that is hidden in the wilderness, finally leading all that remains of Israel on earth to salvation by grace through faith in Him (Rom. 11:26).

There is some evidence that Christ has traveled back and forth between Earth and Heaven during this time period. (In Chapter 14 He appears first on earth with the 144,000 and later in Heaven preparing to reap the harvest of judgment.) At some point before the last battle He returns to Heaven and prepares His truly triumphant ride into Jerusalem.

While the battle ends almost instantly as Christ appears, Zechariah 14 tells us that there will be at least a short period of fighting before He arrives. As all of the nations gather in Jerusalem, they violently terrorize the city (Zech. 14:1-3). The

Lord Jesus Himself will appear, standing on and splitting the Mt. of Olives, making a path of escape for those still alive in Jerusalem. Then Zechariah 14:5 describes exactly what happens in Rev. 19:11-13. **Then the LORD, my God, will come, and all the holy ones with Him!** (Zech. 14:5 NASB).

Revelation 19 tells us that once Christ arrives, there will be no real battle. An angel will call the birds to come gather for the feast, and at Jesus' command someone will seize the beast and false prophet and throw them directly into the Lake of Fire. The rest of the armies will then simply die at a word from the Lord. Zechariah 14:12 (perhaps the inspiration for the climactic scene in "Raiders of the Lost Ark"?) describes what will happen like this:

Now this will be the plague with which the LORD will strike all the peoples who have gone to war against Jerusalem; their flesh will rot while they stand on their feet, and their eyes will rot in their sockets, and their tongue will rot in their mouth. (Zech. 14:12 NASB)

The result will be what John saw in his vision in Rev. 14, blood flowing in the valley as deep as the horses' bridles.

Then, as Zechariah 14:9 proclaims:

And the LORD will be king over all the earth; in that day the LORD will be the only one, and His name the only one. (Zechariah 14:9 NASB)

Thus begins, at long last, the Kingdom promised to Israel for centuries on end. Christ has staked His claim to that throne (and all others), wearing a crown made up of many crowns (Rev. 19:12), perhaps the very one made for Joshua the high priest and kept in the rebuilt temple after the exiles returned to Jerusalem (Zechariah 6:11-15). This crown was designed to prophecy the eventual joining of two offices that had before been kept intentionally separate—the kingship and the priesthood—in the person of Jesus Christ (Hebrews 7). We will look at His 1,000-year kingdom in the next study.

QUESTION 37

What is the Millennial Kingdom?

Read Rev. 20:1-10; Daniel 7:9-14, 21-27

Remember the story of the Kingdom? God, the rightful King, created all that is and gave mankind instructions on how to rule over His creation. He also gave us a choice—to continue under His loving rule in close relationship with Him, or try to rule ourselves. Satan, who had already led a failed rebellion in Heaven, lied to Adam and Eve, convincing them to join his rebellion and rule their own lives. And even as God pronounced judgment on them, He gave them hope, promising that One would come who would defeat the rebel and give them an opportunity to be reborn back into God's Kingdom (Gen. 3:15).

Adam and Eve and their children lived under the consequences of their choice—hard labor, difficult relationships, and eventually sickness and death. Their very first son introduced violence into the mix, killing his righteous brother out of jealousy. Satan continued his battle to destroy humanity, inspiring his fellow rebels to violence against those who repented and became loyal once again to God's Kingdom through faith (Heb. 11). Once God had called out and set aside Israel, Satan particularly focused on destroying them from within (through sin and idolatry) and from without (by enemies and hungry empires), desperately trying to prevent the Savior from coming.

Satan raised up empires led by men as rebellious and prideful as he (Is. 14; Ezekiel 28). These empires began to fight and swallow up each other along with the smaller nations around them. The northern kingdom of Israel was swallowed up by Assyria; the southern kingdom of Judah by Babylon. Media-Persia, Greece, and Rome followed in turn, all keeping Israel under their thumbs. The everlasting Kingdom that God had promised to David and his descendants (1 Chronicles 28:1-8) seemed but a dream.

But God continued to promise this Kingdom to His people, even during their captivity through Ezekiel and Daniel and after their return home through Zechariah. The number and the grandeur of these promises boggles the mind, and would make a long and wonderful Bible study just by themselves. But we will hit only a few highlights here.

First, God promised that when the Kingdom arrived in its fullness, it would usher in a time of complete peace for the nation that has always been troubled by wars and by enemies (Is. 65:18-25). That passage also hints strongly that it will be a time when many of the curses brought into creation through sin will be eliminated or greatly reduced. (For example, Is. 65:20 tells us that lifespans will be greatly expanded, perhaps even to the 900+ years known before the flood).

Second, it will be a time when the nation of Israel is finally the preeminent nation on earth. There will be no more rivals. In fact, non-Jews will come to Jerusalem to learn and to worship (Isaiah 2:1-4; Zechariah 14:16). For this to happen, there will have to be some Gentile survivors after the Battle of Armageddon. As discussed earlier, these will have to be people who did not take the mark of the beast, as all of those are lost and will die at Armageddon (if not from the judgments leading up to that great and final battle—Rev. 14:9-11). But they will also be people who were not saved before the rapture, otherwise they would have been taken then.

God revealed through Daniel that representatives from the nations will survive into the Millennial Kingdom. (**As for the rest of the beasts, their dominion was taken away, but an extension of life was granted to them for an appointed period of time.** Daniel 9:12 NASB) This happens after the little horn, representing anti-Christ, is destroyed—which happens just before the beginning of the Millennial Kingdom. They will have no **dominion**—all authority on earth at that time will reside in Israel. But they will exist, and they will come to Israel to learn.

Third and best of all, God promised that He Himself would reign in Jerusalem at the time of the Kingdom through the Righteous Branch, whom we know to be the glorified Jesus Christ (Is. 11:1-10; Zechariah 2:4-5, 10-13). He will reign as King in Jerusalem, perhaps with the resurrected King David at His side. He will protect Israel personally, just as God did when He accompanied them in the cloud and pillar of fire during the time of the Exodus.

Revelation 20 gives us some additional details about this period in history. First, it tells us that this period of time will last for 1,000 years (the meaning of the word "Millennium"). Second, we learn that Satan, the dragon, will be chained and bound in the very abyss where many of his most terrible demons had been bound for centuries. (We are not told where the demons will be; perhaps they will join him in the abyss or will have already been sent to the Lake of Fire.) This is significant, because it means that the undiluted truth will be known all around the world for the first time since Adam and Eve fell into sin. There will still be disobedience (Zechariah 14:18-19), but it will be perpetrated by those who are fully aware of what they are doing.

Finally, we learn that there will be both mortals and resurrected believers living on Earth together at this time. Here is what Rev. 20:4-6 says:

Then I saw thrones, and they sat on them, and judgment was given to them. And I saw the souls of those who had been beheaded because of their testimony of Jesus and because of the word of God, and those who had not worshiped the beast or his image, and had not received the mark on their forehead and on their hand; and they came to life and reigned with Christ for a thousand years. 5 The rest of the dead did not come to life until the thousand years were completed. This is the first resurrec-

tion. 6 Blessed and holy is the one who has a part in the first resurrection; over these the second death has no power, but they will be priests of God and of Christ and will reign with Him for a thousand years. (NASB)

This is a tricky passage, with a couple of possible interpretations. What we know for certain is that believers who have been martyred for their faith will reign with Christ on earth during the Millennium. This is part of His promise to believers (2 Tim. 2:12). What is less certain is whether only martyrs (and whether this includes only martyrs from the Great Tribulation or from all of history) will reign with Him or whether all believers will have this privilege.

Remember that believers were resurrected when Jesus came at the rapture according to 1 Thessalonians 4:13-18. It could be that martyrs were held back and not resurrected at that time and will experience a special resurrection here. But their resurrection, whether at the rapture or after, is still part of the First Resurrection, which is the resurrection of believers, since eternal life is promised to all who are part of the First Resurrection. Those who will be resurrected after the Millennium is over are primarily the lost. We will look at this resurrection in the next study.

A curious thing happens at the end of the Millennium. Satan is briefly set free and allowed to deceive the nations once again. He is able to assemble a large force which once again marches on Jerusalem. This time, however, they will not be allowed to kill and ravage those inside. God Himself will send fire from Heaven to destroy these forces, and then Satan will receive his eternal judgment in the hottest and deepest part of the Lake of Fire.

What does this show us? It shows us that even without Satan's deception, there is rebellion in the human heart that must be dealt with one way or another. Christ's reign will be perfect, the first perfect ruler in all of human history. And yet some will not like being under His authority. Some nations will refuse to come to Jerusalem to worship at the appointed times and will be punished by being denied needed rain. Apparently a large number of people born to those who enter the Millennial Kingdom will choose not to deal with their rebellion through repentance and faith, but will harbor it in their hearts and respond enthusiastically when the original rebel once again stokes those fires of independence from the authority of the rightful King. So while Satan manipulates the rebellion within us, it is there even when he is not around. We cannot say the Devil made us do anything. He can make sin look much more inviting and much easier to justify. But ultimately we make the choice to either serve God or to serve ourselves.

QUESTION 38

What happens at the Great White Throne?

Read Rev. 20:11-15; 2 Peter 3:10

After the end of the Millennial Kingdom and the final punishment of Satan, Earth and Heaven as we know it will disappear. God the Father, who until this point in time has not left Heaven, will now appear for all to see. An awesome throne will be set up for Him, and from this throne He will conduct the final judgment of humankind.

Once again, some review is in order. Remember that all believers of all ages were resurrected when Christ returned at the rapture. Presumably, these believers have already appeared at the Judgment Seat of Christ and received their rewards (1 Cor. 3:11-15). There is a group, however, which was not resurrected before the Millennium. These are the lost, and they will receive their eternal bodies at this time during the second resurrection.

When these people stand before God, they will face their deeds, all of which are being recorded in books. Does this frighten you a little, to know that God is keeping a record of everything that we do? Jesus clearly warned us that we will one day be called to give an account of all of our deeds and even our words (Luke 12:2-4; Matt. 12:36). When lost rebels who have not repented of their sins stand before God, they will not be able to argue their innocence. The evidence will be clear.

There is one exception, however. If a person's name is

found recorded in a different book—the Book of Life—then this person will not be lost! That does not mean that this person has no sinful deeds or words on their record. But it does mean that their guilt for those sins has been washed away by the blood of Jesus! So at the final judgment, the best and only hope for any sinner is to find his or her name written in that book. And the only way that that can happen is for the person, during his or her lifetime, to repent of sin and rebellion and to believe in Jesus—His sinless life, His sacrificial death, and His resurrection—and to ask to have what He did on the cross applied to us!

Many Bible students teach that this judgment will only be for lost people. It is certainly true that they will be the vast majority of the subjects here. But is it at all possible that there will be some saved people here who do find their names written in the Book of Life? Verse 15 could certainly be taken to imply that there are some here who are in that book. But how could this be? And who would they be?

We are told that life spans are greatly increased during the Millennial Kingdom (Isaiah 65:20), but people will still die during that time. If saved people die during Christ's millennial reign, then they will have to be resurrected at some point. I believe that this may be the time when they also receive their eternal bodies. This would explain why the passage seems to say that there will be some present who are saved.

Two other details bear mentioning here. First, we learn that at least most of those appearing at this judgment come out of Hades. We will discuss this in more detail in the last Flashback, but since Christ's ascension, Hades is now the holding-place for the souls/spirits of the unbelieving dead. Second, we see that death and Hades themselves are both thrown into the Lake of Fire, along with all of those missing from the Book of Life. The Lake of Fire is the eternal place of punishment that we most often call Hell. There is Scriptural evidence that even the lost in Hades are in a place of fire (Luke 16:23-24). But the Lake of Fire is their final destination. This is a very sad fact, and one that will hopefully stoke our own fires for personal evangelism! But there is one small shred of positive news here. The fact that death and Hades are thrown into the Lake of Fire shows that this is their end, as well. Never again will anyone have to say good-bye to a loved one after this point in history! Eternity will be one of truly everlasting life for believers!

The last enemy that will be abolished is death.... But when this perishable will have put on the imperishable, and this mortal will have put on immortality, then will come about the saying that is written, "DEATH IS SWALLOWED UP in victory. "O DEATH, WHERE IS YOUR VICTORY? O DEATH, WHERE IS YOUR STING?" The sting of death is sin, and the power of sin is the law; but thanks be to God, who gives us the victory through our Lord Jesus Christ. Therefore, my beloved brethren, be steadfast, immovable, always abounding in the work of the Lord, knowing that your toil is not in vain in the Lord. (1 Cor. 15:26, 54-58 NASB)

QUESTION 39

What does it mean that God will make all things new?

Read Revelation 21:1-22:9

Heaven and Earth had disappeared during the great white throne judgment; now John sees a new Heaven and a new Earth. He notes that oceans are no more. Many of us might be tempted to see just a tiny note of sadness in that remark, but considering what God has promised us about eternity (Rom. 8:18), that is doubtful. As much as many of us love the beach, we must remember that the oceans are a testimony to the most terrible judgment that has ever fallen on the earth. The oceans are all that remain of the worldwide flood from Noah's day.

John also sees the chief city of the new Earth—New Jerusalem—coming down from Heaven. This is the place where Jesus is even now creating dwelling places for His children (John 14:2-3). Most of the rest of this section sets out to describe the New Jerusalem, but before that happens, John makes a very important declaration. It is more wonderful than any of the amazing truths about the Heavenly city that follow. God has come down to live with His people. He will live with them forever, comforting the hurts of their past and drying their tears. Forever. Walls of jasper and streets of gold are amazing, as are the dimensions of the city itself. But the most important thing about eternity is that God is there, and that we will always be with Him.

One of the angels who poured out one of the final bowl

judgments then takes John on a personal tour of the eternal city! First, he sees that the city reflects the same glory that he had seen around the Father in the throne room. It glows like the purest of diamonds. Second, he notices that it has 12 gates, each bearing the name of one of the sons of Israel, and 12 foundation stones, each bearing the name of one of the apostles. This emphasizes the essential parts that both of these groups played in the salvation of everyone who will dwell in the city. This is also a very strong clue, I believe, that the 24 elders are these two groups of redeemed men.

The foundation stones are adorned with the most valuable jewels, and each gate is a giant pearl! The walls are like diamonds and streets are purest transparent gold. And the dimensions of the city are incredible. It is a cube that stretches 1500 miles in every direction, including up into the sky! This great city would stretch from Denver, CO almost to Washington, DC, and from Houston, TX to Winnipeg, Manitoba! It will have room for many multitudes of believers. And its incredible size may indicate that the new Earth will be much larger than the current one. Unlike the Jerusalem of this age, it will have no temple, since God will be available to meet with everyone and will no longer need to be veiled. It will always be daytime, and the glory of the Father and Son will be its source of light. Its gates will always be open, and no evil will ever come through those gates. Only those who have been saved will ever enter there.

Inside the city, a river of the water of life, just like Jesus promised to the woman at the well (John 4:10) and to all believers (John 7:38), will flow from the thrones of Father and Son. (And do not think that the Holy Spirit is left out here; John 7:39 tells us that He Himself is the water of life for believers!) God is the source of all life, including eternal life. Water shortages were always a threat in ancient Israel; the new Earth will experience none of those. Impressive fruit trees with healing leaves line the golden street. And there is no hint of any of the things that came along with the curse brought by our sin—no darkness, no pain, no grief, no burning sun, no thirst, no hunger, and best of all, no death. Never again will these things touch the lives of God's people!

The Bible gives us only small glimpses of Heaven—of Heaven now and of the new Heaven and Earth to come. But the few details that it does give us show us that it will be a place beyond anything we could imagine here on earth. Some of the things that we value the most here on earth will be its construction materials. And the presence of God—Father, Son, and Spirit —will be full and uninterrupted. God has indeed planned something that will more than make up for our worst suffering here on earth (Rom. 8:18). And that is not making light of the suffering, which is very real. It is simply emphasizing the awesomeness of what awaits us!

So when God says He is making all things new, it does not mean that there will not be anything that we recognize or that is tied to the past. But all of these things will be like they were originally intended to be before sin corrupted them—or better! Probably a lot like what He has done for us. When He saves us, He makes us new creations in Christ. This does not mean that we cease to be us, but it means that Christ changes us to make us who we were originally created us to be.

FLASHBACK 10

The History of Heaven

Read Luke 16:19-31; Philippians 1:23-24; Rev. 21:3-4

Well-meaning preachers—this one included—often talk about Heaven without clearly explaining its history. For example, we may picture our departed loved ones walking streets of gold in a land of no more tears. But are all of these things descriptions of Heaven as it exists now? And have believers always gone to the current Heaven when they died?

We tend to think of Heaven as having always existed as God's home. But the Bible gives us some details that provide a different picture. First of all, while God, of course, has always existed (Ps. 90:2; 93:2), Heaven has not! Genesis 1:1 says: **In the beginning God created the heavens and the earth** (NASB). The Hebrews counted three different heavens: the First Heaven, roughly equivalent to the earth's atmosphere; the Second Heaven, what we might call outer space; and the Third Heaven (2 Cor. 12:2), where God's throne is. This Third Heaven is the one that we are usually thinking about when we use that word.

The current Heaven is the one described in most of the book of Revelation, although the events that we see are yet future. And while this is no doubt the Heaven that was created in the beginning, it has not always been the immediate destination of believers at their deaths.

Jesus gives us some first-hand information about the place of the dead (called "Sheol" in the Old Testament and "Hades" in the New) in Luke 16. He describes two men, one a rich man and the other a poor beggar named Lazarus. Both men die and go to Sheol/Hades, but find themselves in very different situations. Lazarus is safe and comforted in the bosom of Abraham, the father of men and women of faith (Gal. 3:6-7), while the rich man is in a place of burning torment. There is communication between the two places, but no possibility of crossing over between one and the other.

Two things are very clear in Jesus' story. The eternal destinies of Old Testament believers and unbelievers were set at death, dependent upon whether or not each person chose to exercise faith (Heb. 11). But even believers were not yet welcomed into Heaven to be in God's presence. Why would this be the case? Because Jesus had not yet completed His work of atonement. Hebrews 10:4 tells us that animal blood was not enough to pay for human sin. Until Jesus died on the cross, our sins could not be permanently covered, and so we could not live in Heaven with God. But after Jesus' death and resurrection, the souls/spirits of Old Testament believers could go into God's presence, and this happened to those in Abraham's bosom when He ascended (Eph. 4:8).

The details given to us by Jesus in this passage also help to explain another Biblical mystery. You will remember that Jesus promised the thief on the cross that they would be together that very day in Paradise (Luke 23:43). But Peter tells us that, after His death, Jesus visited and preached to spirits in prison (1 Peter 3:18-20). How can both be true? Since before His ascension both places were in Sheol/Hades, and since there was communication between the two, this means that Jesus was in Abraham's bosom —at that time also called Paradise—from which He could make His proclamation to those spirits who were in torment alongside the rich man! Further confirming that Jesus did not go to Heaven after His death is His declaration to Mary Magdalene after His resurrection that He had not yet returned to His Father in Heaven (John 20:17).

We know that since Jesus' ascension the souls/spirits of believers who die do go directly to Heaven (where Paradise was also taken—2 Cor. 12:4) to be with Jesus (Phil. 1:23; 2 Cor. 5:8) while our bodies sleep, awaiting the resurrection (1 Thess. 4:13-18). But what is Heaven like right now? Do our loved ones who are there walk on streets of gold? Have all tears and sorrow completely come to an end?

Rev. 6:9 gives us one of the few glimpses of believers in the current Heaven. Did you notice that, while they are being comforted by God and are completely safe in His care, they are not completely satisfied with the current state of the universe? They are begging God to bring the persecution of their loved ones on Earth to an end and to take control of His Kingdom once again. His response is that they must wait just a little while longer.

Is this the picture that we usually have of our loved ones in Heaven? Please do not misunderstand. Our loved ones are in complete joy (Ps. 16:11). They know no physical suffering and no fear for their future. But they are not completely satisfied. Like the angels and the other inhabitants of Heaven, they want to see God take His rightful rule of the universe once more. They want to see the enemy defeated and all believers together with the Lord. And no doubt they also eagerly await their resurrected bodies and the future that God has prepared for us.

It is actually not until after the rapture (Rev. 7:16-17) when an end to all tears and grief is promised to believers individually, and finally in the New Jerusalem (Rev. 21:3-4)—after the conclusion of the Millennial Kingdom and destruction of the first heavens and Earth--when a final end to all of these things and to death itself is proclaimed. Paul tells us that death is the very last enemy that will be destroyed (1 Cor. 15:26). It is also with the descent of the New Jerusalem onto the New Earth that we get the gates of pearl and streets of gold. So while Heaven is already an awesome place, especially because God is there, it is not now the final version of itself. That awaits the end of this current universe after the Millennium.

QUESTION 40

What's all this about Jesus coming
quickly? Did we miss something??

Read Revelation 22:6-7, 10; 2 Peter 3:3-9; Revelation 1:3

Three words appear in the first and last chapters of Revelation that might make us wonder a little: **near**, **soon**, and **quickly** —all in reference to Christ's return. It is fair to ask why these words were used more than 1,900 years ago since Christ still has not come back. (Of course, all of us who are doing this study now can be thankful, since we would not have existed if He had not delayed!)

Some people, in fact, claim that the events of Revelation have actually occurred. These folks, known as Preterists, take these three words quite literally, arguing that the events described in the Bible's last book had to have happened in John's lifetime if these passages are to be believed. Of course, this position makes it difficult to take most of the rest of Revelation literally, since there is no historical record of the signs in the Heavens, 100 lb hailstones, the release of terrible demons from the abyss, or the visible return of Christ in the sky. So while I respect the desire of preterists to take these verses seriously, I believe a lot more violence is done to a lot more Scripture by taking that position.

One thing that we should find encouraging is that skeptics in the First Century were already asking, "What's taking Him so long?" Peter addresses this very situation in 2 Peter 3, and thankfully he also provides us with what I believe is the answer to our question. Peter tells First Century believers that God's definition of "soon" or "quickly" is different from ours. Because He is eternal, He sees little difference in 10,000 years or a single day. We, on the other hand, see a great deal of difference, especially since our life spans rarely stretch to even 100 years. This is a case where God's definition of those words is different from ours, and we can take it on faith that God was using His definition rather than ours. This does not mean that the words have no meaning. For the eternal God, 2,000 years (or however many it turns out to be) do make up just a tiny blip in time.

But there is something else in this passage from 2 Peter that we should understand. As with everything the Father does, there is a very important reason behind His delay. It is the desire of His heart for everyone who will repent of their rebellion and believe in Jesus for salvation to have that opportunity. He knows the last person who will trust Christ as Savior in this age of the world, and He knows when that person will make his or her decision. And because of His great love and mercy for His creatures, He will not allow the end to come one moment before this person has trusted Christ and received His gift of salvation. He will not allow anyone who is willing to be saved to miss out on that opportunity!

So this is one of those cases where we have to trust both God's wisdom and His heart. Skeptics will continue to challenge His math, and God will allow them to do so rather than deny someone an opportunity for salvation. Of course, He is also showing mercy on the skeptics by delaying, since His return will bring God's wrath on the unbelieving world. Perhaps one of these skeptics will even turn out to be the last person who comes to salvation! That would be so much like our loving Heavenly Father!

QUESTION 41

How does Revelation end?

Read Revelation 22:10-21

Not surprisingly, the book of Revelation ends with two invitations. After a long and detailed description of the last seven years of world history, capped with a shorter description of the Millennium, the final judgment, and the New Jerusalem, the focus comes back to the focus of the heart of God and the heart of His true church: preparing hearts and lives for the events that will surely come.

Right on the heels of yet another promise that the time is near, God once again makes a clear distinction between those who are prepared—**those who wash their robes** (Rev. 22:14 NASB) in the blood of the Lamb and those who will not (Rev. 22:15). A joint invitation is offered by the Holy Spirit, who convicts the world of its need (John 16:8) and the church who, by the Spirit's wisdom and power, shares the Gospel message and its own testimony of salvation by grace through faith in Jesus (Eph. 2:8-10; Acts 1:8). The invitation is for anyone who is thirsty to **take the water of life without cost** (Rev. 22:17 NASB).

Then, in the last verse, a second invitation is offered. After yet another reminder that Jesus' return is near, John himself, his spirit groaning within him (Rom. 8:23), agrees and begs His Lord to come! To come back and take His throne. To come back and rescue His church. To come back and fulfill all of His wonderful promises to His children.

Paul echoed this invitation in 1 Cor. 16:22. After pronouncing a curse on those who do not love the Lord, he prays the one word Aramaic prayer commonly prayed by early believers—**Maranatha**. That prayer means, "O, Lord, come!" This has been the prayer of the church since its beginning. Only in times when the church has become too comfortable in Babylon has the urgency of that prayer been hindered. And whenever that has happened, God has once again called His people to come out of that rebel kingdom, prodding them with uncomfortable things such as persecution if necessary. The true church will always be eager to see Christ return (2 Timothy 4:8), even with the terrible events that must happen before He does. My prayer is that, after having studied some of these things in more depth, you will feel more than ever the urgency of this prayer, and the need to dig deeply into all the Scriptures for strength and understanding.

The grace of the Lord Jesus be with all. Amen.
(Rev. 22:21 NASB)

Made in the USA
Middletown, DE
25 March 2019